DISEASES AND DISORDERS

LYME DISEASE
WHEN TICKS MAKE YOU SICK

By Raymond J. Lampke

Portions of this book originally appeared in *Lyme Disease* by Shannon Kelly.

LUCENT
PRESS

Published in 2019 by
Lucent Press, an Imprint of Greenhaven Publishing, LLC
353 3rd Avenue
Suite 255
New York, NY 10010

Designer: Deanna Paternostro
Editor: Jennifer Lombardo

Library of Congress Cataloging-in-Publication Data

Names: Lampke, Raymond J., author.
Title: Lyme disease : when ticks make you sick / Raymond J. Lampke.
Description: New York : Lucent Press, [2019] | Series: Diseases and disorders
   | Includes bibliographical references and index.
Identifiers: LCCN 2018004777 (print) | LCCN 2018010596 (ebook) | ISBN
   9781534563636 (eBook) | ISBN 9781534563629 (library bound book) | ISBN
   9781534563643 (paperback)
Subjects: LCSH: Lyme disease.
Classification: LCC RA644.L94 (ebook) | LCC RA644.L94 L36 2019 (print) | DDC
   614.5/746–dc23
LC record available at https://lccn.loc.gov/2018004777

Printed in the United States of America

CPSIA compliance information: Batch #BS18KL: For further information contact Greenhaven Publishing LLC, New York,
New York at 1-844-317-7404.

Please visit our website, www.greenhavenpublishing.com. For a free color catalog of all our
high-quality books, call toll free 1-844-317-7404 or fax 1-844-317-7405.

CONTENTS

Illness is an unfortunate part of life, and it is one that is often misunderstood. Thanks to advances in science and technology, people have been aware for many years that diseases such as the flu, pneumonia, and chicken pox are caused by viruses and bacteria. These diseases all cause physical symptoms that people can see and understand, and many people have dealt with these diseases themselves. However, sometimes diseases that were previously unknown in most of the world turn into epidemics and spread across the globe. Without an awareness of the method by which these diseases are spread—through the air, through human waste or fluids, through sexual contact, or by some other method—people cannot take the proper precautions to prevent further contamination. Panic often accompanies epidemics as a result of this lack of knowledge.

Knowledge is power in the case of mental disorders, as well. Mental disorders are just as common as physical disorders, but due to a lack of awareness among the general public, they are often stigmatized. Scientists have studied them for years and have found that they are generally caused by hormonal imbalances in the brain, but they have not yet determined with certainty what causes those imbalances or how to fix them. Because even mild mental illness is stigmatized in Western society, many people prefer not to talk about it.

Chronic pain disorders are also not well understood—even by researchers—and do not yet have foolproof treatments. People who have a mental disorder or a disease or disorder that causes them to feel chronic pain can be the target of uninformed opinions. People who do not have these disorders sometimes struggle to understand how difficult it can be to deal with the symptoms. These disorders are often termed "invisible illnesses" because no one can see the symptoms; this leads many people to doubt that they exist or are serious problems. Additionally, people who have an undiagnosed disorder may understand that they are experiencing the world in a different way than their peers, but they have no one to turn to for answers.

Misinformation about all kinds of ailments is often spread through personal anecdotes, social media, and even news sources. This series aims to present accurate information about both physical and mental conditions so young adults will have a better understanding of them. Each volume discusses the symptoms of a particular disease or disorder, ways it is currently being treated, and the research that is being done to understand it further. Advice for people who may be suffering from a disorder is included, as well as information for their loved ones about how best to support them.

With fully cited quotes, a list of recommended books and websites for further research, and informational charts, this series provides young adults with a factual introduction to common illnesses. By learning more about these ailments, they will be better able to prevent the spread of contagious diseases, show compassion to people who are dealing with invisible illnesses, and take charge of their own health.

INTRODUCTION

"REMOVING THE NAILS"

From the beginning of a doctor's path through medical school, they are generally taught to establish a single root cause of a patient's discomfort. They will piece together clues from a patient's symptoms and any changes in the way the body looks to narrow down the possibilities of what it might be. Diagnostic tools such as blood work and medical imaging can give them a logical conclusion: the diagnosis.

However, what if the symptoms presented to a physician are numerous? What if these symptoms are similar to the ones seen in many common diseases? If the etiology (the cause of a patient's symptoms) was varied, constantly changing, and concerned every major body system, how many different diagnoses might each specialist develop? These questions reflect the problems of diagnosing and treating patients who have been touched by Lyme disease.

"Think of chronic illness as a patient with sixteen nails in his or her foot," wrote Dr. Richard Horowitz, a respected Lyme disease expert, researcher, and author of the book *Why Can't I Get Better?* He continued,

> Their physician might identify several nails in their workup and treat those specific causes, but often, if they do not achieve a positive result by pulling out one of those nails, they believe they have erred in their diagnosis. However, this does not mean they were wrong … It is essential to look further and find all of the nails.[1]

6

Lyme disease is spread to humans through ticks—small insects that live on animals, especially wild ones such as deer. It is the most common tick-borne illness in North America and Europe and has been found on almost every continent. It has been classified as an emerging disease due to the increasing number of cases seen each year and its geographic spread. Over 38,000 cases were confirmed in the United States in 2015. Lyme disease is often misdiagnosed, however, and the Centers for Disease Control and Prevention (CDC) estimates that only 10 percent of probable Lyme disease cases are diagnosed correctly. The CDC also noted that underreporting could put the actual count at 300,000 cases.

Lyme disease is a multifaceted illness. Disagreements that occur among medical professionals have left patients in a difficult situation. Often, many doctors are seen and numerous referrals are given in a long cycle of misdiagnosis and anxiety. Patients may become viewed as challenging by doctors when their complex symptoms do not correspond with common illnesses.

While the greatest concentration of Lyme disease diagnoses in the United States can be found in the northeastern region of the country—96 percent of the reported cases are located in just 14 states—every state except Hawaii—has reported at least one case in recent years. However, because so many cases occur in so few states, many people remain uninformed about the disease.

Since the late 1990s, Lyme has expanded from small pockets in Connecticut, New York, Massachusetts, and New Jersey to confirmed cases throughout the Midwest and California, and into Canada. The disease's spread is cause for concern among the medical community at large and has prompted further study. Within the last decade, through the efforts of dedicated clinicians and researchers, the pieces of the Lyme disease puzzle are beginning to fit into place.

Still, the lack of effective standardized medical testing for the disease has been a major contributor to the mystery of Lyme disease. The symptoms are confusing—there are many of them, and two people with Lyme disease may show completely different symptoms. This has made Lyme disease patients less of a priority than those with more well-known and easily diagnosable diseases, such as breast cancer or heart disease. It has also made the cost of care too high for many to afford, as they undergo multiple tests that their health insurance may not cover, and it has also affected the lives of patients who have had their illness misdiagnosed.

It is important for people who enter wooded or grassy areas to be aware of the possibility of being bitten by a tick that may carry Lyme disease.

The bacterium responsible for causing Lyme infection was not discovered until 1981. It was a decade later, in 1991, that Lyme became a nationally reportable disease in the United States, which means that doctors are required to report all cases to their county or state public health department. As with all complex illnesses, research and devoted clinical response to fight the disease is crucial. The manner in which the disease is treated has led to arguments among established medical institutions and has seen the rise of a creative new patient-centered association of doctors who aggressively treat Lyme based on the individual symptoms of the patient. More than 25 years since the disease was first documented in medical literature, increased awareness, activism, and political interest has sped up the search for better methods of treating and preventing Lyme disease in communities, with a watchful eye toward improved tests for diagnosing the disease and perhaps the ultimate goals—a cure and a vaccine.

CHAPTER ONE

UNDERSTANDING LYME DISEASE

Lyme disease is an illness transmitted by ticks that is considered by most doctors to be easy to treat if caught early. However, it can cause serious problems if left undiagnosed for a long time. Although Lyme disease cases have appeared in nearly every state in the United States and in many other areas around the world, people who live, work, or travel in certain areas are more likely to be exposed than others. Knowing the facts about where the disease comes from and how it is passed to humans can help people take precautions to prevent getting infected.

Lyme disease is a bacterial illness. Bacteria are single-celled microscopic organisms that can be found in almost every environment on the planet. Most bacteria are harmless—in fact, less than 1 percent of bacteria cause disease. The human body contains hundreds of species of bacteria that generally cause no difficulties and often have useful functions, such as helping in the digestion of food. The bacteria that do cause illnesses are referred to as pathogens, and they can be spread through air, food, water, contaminated soil, or close physical contact with an infected person. Other pathogens are spread through the bite of an infected insect such as a flea, mite, or tick.

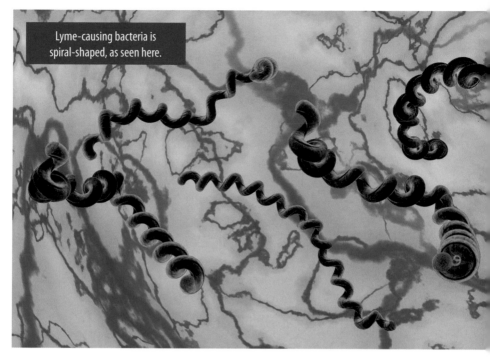

Lyme-causing bacteria is spiral-shaped, as seen here.

Route of Infection

Lyme disease is classified as a zoonosis—a viral or bacterial disease that can be passed from animals to humans. It is caused by approximately one-third of the members of the bacteria genus *Borrelia* (abbreviated as *B.*), which are members of the spirochete family. Spirochetes are long and slender with a distinctive coiled shape. A strain of *Borrelia* known as *B. burgdorferi* sensu stricto is responsible for the majority of Lyme disease cases in the United States, while *B. garinii* and *B. afzelii* account for most European cases. All strains of *Borrelia* that can cause Lyme disease are referred to collectively as *B. burgdorferi* sensu lato. Due to its Latin name, Lyme disease is also sometimes referred to as Lyme borreliosis.

Lyme disease is a vector-borne disease, which means it is transmitted from one host to another by a vector, or carrier. While humans become infected with *B. burgdorferi* sensu lato bacteria through the bite of a tick, the tick is not the original host of the bacteria; it is the vector. This is because although the bacteria are carried inside the tick's body and transmitted through its bite, the tick does not develop symptoms of the disease. A tick becomes infected with the bacteria when it feeds on a source that naturally carries a Lyme-causing strain of *Borrelia*, such as a chipmunk, shrew, or mouse. The bacteria are then carried by the tick. When the infected tick bites a person and begins to feed on their blood, *Borrelia* spirochetes are transferred from the tick through its saliva and into the person's bloodstream.

Hard ticks, known by the Latin name *Ixodidae*, are responsible for the transmission of Lyme disease to humans. In the eastern United States, the main culprit is the black-legged tick (*Ixodes scapularis*), while in the West, it is the western black-legged tick (*Ixodes pacificus*). The eastern black-legged tick is also known as the deer tick, as the deer is one of its major food sources. The main vector in Europe is the castor bean or sheep tick (*Ixodes ricinus*), and in Asia, it is the taiga tick (*Ixodes persulcatus*).

Ticks typically come into contact with *B. burgdorferi* sensu lato bacteria before they reach maturity. Ticks emerge from their eggs as larvae. A larva then takes a blood meal from a small host, which may be infected with the bacteria. After this first meal, a larva will not eat again until it has moved into the next stage in its life cycle: the nymph. Therefore, there is very little chance that a human can become infected with Lyme disease by being bitten by a tick larva. The only way this could occur is if the bacteria had been transmitted from an infected adult tick to its eggs, which is a rare occurrence.

During its nymph stage, a tick may also feed on an infected animal host or a human. This is when ticks are most dangerous to humans. Nymphs are extremely tiny—a black-legged tick nymph is only about the size of a poppy seed or the head of a pin—and their bite is typically painless. A person can easily have a nymph attached to their skin and not realize it for a prolonged period of time. Time is a key concern in the transmission of Lyme disease, as it takes approximately 36 to 48 hours for the spirochetes to transfer from the tick to its human host. If a tick is removed from the skin before this time period has passed, it is less likely that the person will develop Lyme disease, but it is still wise to seek medical attention with the discovery of any embedded tick. It is also a good idea for people with symptoms of Lyme disease to talk to a doctor even if they have not found a tick on their body. According to LymeDisease.org, only 25 percent of Lyme patients remember getting a tick bite.

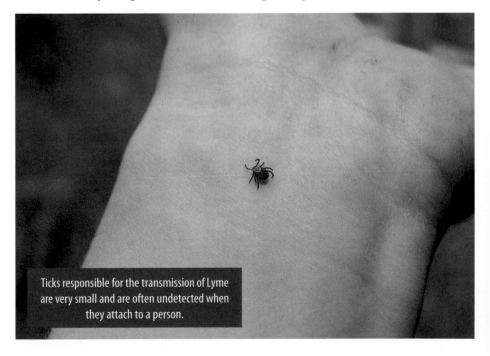

Ticks responsible for the transmission of Lyme are very small and are often undetected when they attach to a person.

The Bacterial Culprit

The spirochete family of bacteria is a relatively small one, made up of only six members. Depending on the species, a spirochete can range in length from five millionths to several hundred millionths of an inch. Most of them move with the use of unique flagella called axial filaments, which are located within the bacterium's cell wall. When the spirochete rotates its axial filaments, it moves in a corkscrew fashion.

Aside from *Borrelia*, two other types of spirochete can cause illness in humans. The best known of this group, *Treponema pallidum*, is responsible for the sexually transmitted disease syphilis. The *Treponema* bacteria cause sores, and the disease is spread when an uninfected person comes into direct contact with these sores during sexual intercourse. Other *Treponema* spirochetes cause less well-known illnesses, such as the diseases yaws and pinta, both of which cause sores to develop on the skin.

Human-to-Human Transmission

According to the CDC, there is no evidence that Lyme disease can be spread through touching or kissing. The CDC also states that the disease cannot be contracted through sexual contact, although some doctors who treat Lyme patients do not think this is an absolute certainty. One factor that confuses the issue is that the bacterium that causes the sexually transmitted disease syphilis, *Treponema pallidum*, is also a spirochete. However, further research is needed to establish whether the ways they are spread are similar. The syphilis bacteria remain close to the surface of the skin in sores, whereas *Borrelia* bacteria hide deep inside the body.

If a woman contracts Lyme disease during pregnancy and she is not properly treated, there is a risk the placenta—the organ that transfers nutrients from the mother to the baby while it is in the womb—could become infected and the fetus could suffer organ damage or die in the womb. In addition, *B. burgdorferi* sensu stricto spirochetes have been discovered in the urine and breast milk of mothers with Lyme disease. In another example of differing opinions in the medical community, while the CDC asserts there are no reports of the disease being transmitted to breastfed children, well-known pediatric Lyme disease specialist Charles Ray Jones, who has treated thousands of children with the condition, claims to know of several babies that he says were infected through breast milk.

Patients undergoing treatment for Lyme disease should not donate blood, as *Borrelia* spirochetes have been found to survive the blood purification process to which donations are subjected. Blood banks may require a waiting period after the end date of the treatment or after active symptoms have passed before allowing someone to donate blood, even if they are no longer infected.

Dangerous Environments

Three major environmental factors that affect whether or not ticks will thrive in a particular area are vegetation, climate, and the availability of a food source. The majority of tick species prefer temperate climates with high humidity at ground level. They are mostly found in deciduous woodlands with a covering of dead leaves or underbrush on the ground. (Deciduous trees are those that shed their leaves seasonally, such as maples.) Ticks can survive in coniferous forests, however, as long as there is enough ground cover and moisture. (Coniferous trees are those that produce cones and have needle-like leaves, such as pines.) Ticks can also be found in grassy dunes, though rarely on open sandy beaches. Areas prone to droughts or flooding are not good environments for ticks.

A large supply of hosts to feed from must also be present. In the larval and nymphal stages, ticks tend to feed on birds and rodents. Adult ticks seek out larger mammals such as deer, cows, or horses. Ticks also feed on reptiles and amphibians such as snakes, lizards, and turtles.

Forested areas with relatively few trees and a high level of human activity, similar to the path shown here, often have a higher number of ticks than deep, dense woodland areas.

Forest areas with few trees often contain more ticks than deeper, dense woodlands. This lack of trees is often due to human activity, which can

Spreading Lyme Disease

Zoonoses are diseases that can be passed from animals to humans. Bacteria, viruses, parasites, and other disease-causing organisms cause zoonotic disease. The World Health Organization (WHO) reports that at least 200 zoonoses have been identified.

The method through which a zoonosis can be transmitted to humans can vary. Some are spread by direct contact with an infected animal, such as being bitten by a dog or bat carrying rabies. Sometimes the feces of an infected animal can contaminate a water supply, and a person who drinks the water falls ill. Other zoonotic pathogens are spread when a person eats the meat from an infected animal. Tapeworms and salmonella are contracted this way. As is the case with Lyme disease, some zoonoses are spread when an insect bites an infected animal and then bites a human. One well-known example of a zoonosis spread this way is the plague. In the 14th century, more than 20 million people were killed as the bubonic plague, known as the Black Death, was spread throughout Europe by infected fleas and rats.

The treatment of a zoonosis naturally depends on the specific disease. Preventive measures include vaccination against zoonotic diseases, cooking food thoroughly before eating, and ensuring a secure and clean water supply.

Ticks such as the one shown here often carry zoonotic pathogens.

create an imbalanced ecosystem. Smaller wooded areas tend to have fewer predator species of animals, which means that small rodents, one of the main food supplies for ticks, can be found in larger numbers. Thus, ever-expanding suburban communities can become as dangerous as, if not more dangerous than, the undeveloped, pure wilds of nature. According to microbiologist Alan G. Barbour, "Associating the risk of Lyme disease exclusively with hiking or hunting in the backwoods or wilderness regions is a misconception. Comparatively few people become infected through recreational activities in remote or otherwise unpopulated areas."[2]

Where Lyme Strikes Hardest

In the United States, there are two major generalized hotspots for Lyme disease: the upper East Coast and a section of the upper Midwest, particularly Minnesota and Wisconsin. Infected ticks are also common along some areas of the California and Oregon coastlines. According to data from the CDC, in 2015, the state with the most confirmed cases of Lyme disease was Pennsylvania, with 9,048. New Jersey had 4,855 confirmed cases, and New York was in third place

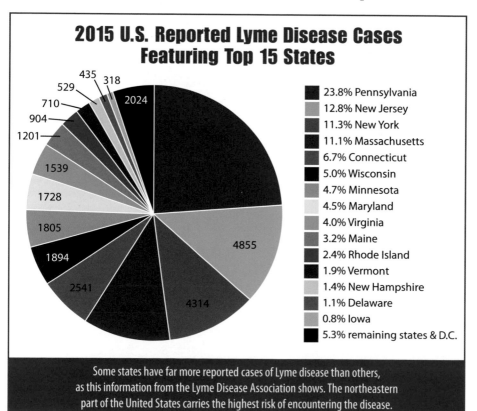

2015 U.S. Reported Lyme Disease Cases Featuring Top 15 States

- 23.8% Pennsylvania
- 12.8% New Jersey
- 11.3% New York
- 11.1% Massachusetts
- 6.7% Connecticut
- 5.0% Wisconsin
- 4.7% Minnesota
- 4.5% Maryland
- 4.0% Virginia
- 3.2% Maine
- 2.4% Rhode Island
- 1.9% Vermont
- 1.4% New Hampshire
- 1.1% Delaware
- 0.8% Iowa
- 5.3% remaining states & D.C.

Some states have far more reported cases of Lyme disease than others, as this information from the Lyme Disease Association shows. The northeastern part of the United States carries the highest risk of encountering the disease.

with 4,314. Up to 50 percent of adult ticks have been found to be infected with *B. burgdorferi* sensu stricto bacteria in the areas of the country that see the most cases.

In Europe, many reported cases occur in the central countries such as Austria, the Czech Republic, Germany, Slovakia, Slovenia, and Switzerland. The number of incidents is likely to increase throughout the continent, however, as recent studies have revealed that significant numbers of ticks examined in other countries are infected with Lyme-causing bacteria. England, Wales, Scotland, and Northern Ireland have all seen an alarming rise in the number of reported cases of Lyme in the last decade. According to a report by the World Health Organization (WHO) and European Centre for Disease Prevention and Control (ECDC), more than 360,000 cases have been reported in Europe in the last 20 years.

In Canada, Lyme disease only became a nationally reportable disease in 2010. The medical professionals that diagnose Lyme must report them to an official medical agency in Canada. Since Lyme disease is only a very recent focus of research in Canada, access to care is limited. Many patients travel to the United States, where treatments are more widely accepted and understood. These patients must then deal with a larger out-of-pocket cost due to international insurance restrictions.

Understanding Tick Development

Ticks that can carry *B. burgdorferi* sensu lato tend to have similar life cycles worldwide, and this information can help determine when humans are at the most risk of infection.

A tick's life has four distinct stages: egg, larval, nymphal, and adult. A female adult tick lays a batch of thousands of eggs in the spring and then dies. The eggs hatch later in the summer into larvae, which have six legs and are extremely tiny—about the size of the period at the end of this sentence. The activity of larvae reaches its peak in August in the Northeast and upper Midwest regions of the United States. After a larva takes its initial blood meal at this stage, it molts into a nymph. Nymphs remain inactive during the winter and early spring, emerging to seek the tick's second blood meal in May. Nymphal activity is highest from late May through July in the United States.

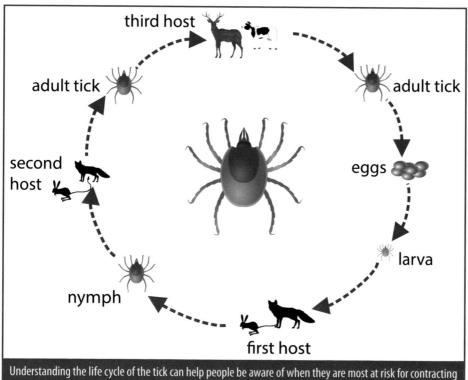

third host

adult tick

adult tick

second host

eggs

larva

nymph

first host

Understanding the life cycle of the tick can help people be aware of when they are most at risk for contracting Lyme disease and take precautions against it.

After its second blood meal, the nymph molts again and develops into an adult tick, which spends the fall seeking a third and final blood meal. The height of adult tick activity in the Lyme disease hotspots in the United States is late October. If the tick is unsuccessful in finding a food source, it will burrow into dead leaves or undergrowth and remain inactive through the winter. When temperatures rise above 45 degrees Fahrenheit (7.2 degrees Celsius), the tick reemerges to resume its quest for a meal. Although this generally does not happen until spring, ticks can be active on warm winter days as well.

Mating is possible for ticks of the *Ixodidae* family—including the black-legged, castor bean, and taiga ticks—only until the adult female finishes her third and final blood meal. Mating may take place on the ground, but it takes place more frequently when the female tick is attached to a host. Once mating is complete and the female has taken her last meal, she drops to the ground, lays her eggs, and dies. The male also dies after reproduction. The tick eggs hatch in the summer, and the cycle begins again.

Lyme disease can be contracted any time of the year that ticks are active, but the majority of infections in the United States occur in May through August. Milder and shorter winters due to climate change over the last several decades have led to an earlier onset of tick activity. Most host-seeking activity takes place in spring and as well as the early summer, with some areas experiencing slight spikes in late summer and fall. According to the American Lyme Disease Foundation (ALDF), individuals with an increased risk of contracting Lyme disease are people who live or vacation in areas where Lyme is a known risk or engage in any occupation or activity that puts them in contact with overgrown vegetation. Occupations that the organization lists as particularly at risk include landscaping, land surveying, forestry, and utility work.

Discovering Lyme

Lyme disease was first officially identified in the United States in the 1970s in the small town of Lyme, Connecticut. The first person to gain attention for the disease was a local artist named Polly Murray. By 1975, Murray had been suffering for 10 years with rashes, headaches, swollen joints, memory loss, nausea, and fatigue (extreme tiredness). Doctors could find no explanation for these symptoms, eventually informing her that her symptoms were all in her head. Three of her children were also battling similar symptoms, and one son had been diagnosed with juvenile idiopathic arthritis (formerly known as juvenile rheumatoid arthritis), a chronic disease that causes children's joints to become painful and swollen. Desperate for answers after the doctors could not help her, Murray began questioning neighbors. She discovered that several other children in the town had also been diagnosed with juvenile idiopathic arthritis. The disease is relatively rare, so it was unusual to have so many children in one area diagnosed with it. For this reason, Murray contacted the Connecticut Department of Public Health.

The health department called upon Allen Steere of Yale University to investigate what was happening in Lyme. Steere was a rheumatologist—a doctor who studies diseases of the joints, bones, and muscles. He determined that the illness was not juvenile idiopathic arthritis. He observed that this disease seemed to strike during specific times of the year and in specific areas in the community. His investigation led him to believe the disease was being transmitted by ticks. When it became clear that patients were developing multiple symptoms that affected the whole body, not just the joints, what had until then been referred to as Lyme arthritis

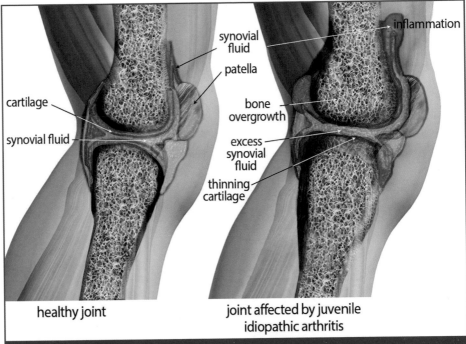

synovial
fluid

patella

inflammation

cartilage

bone
overgrowth

synovial fluid

excess
synovial
fluid

thinning
cartilage

healthy joint

joint affected by juvenile
idiopathic arthritis

Juvenile idiopathic arthritis causes pain and inflammation in children's joints. Its symptoms are similar to those of Lyme disease, which can lead doctors to make a misdiagnosis.

became known as Lyme disease.

The actual spirochete responsible for Lyme was not discovered until 1981, when Willy Burgdorfer, a microbiologist at the National Institutes of Health's Rocky Mountain Laboratories in Montana, received tick samples from the Long Island area of New York State from a colleague. Burgdorfer dissected the ticks and found that 60 percent of them contained a strain of spirochete bacteria in their abdomen. Suspecting he had found the cause of Lyme disease, he established four criteria for scientists to determine whether or not Lyme disease is caused by this spirochete bacterium:

- The bacterium must be present in every case of the disease.
- The bacterium must be isolated (separated) from the diseased host and grown in pure

culture (this means being able to make the isolated bacterium—and only that bacterium—multiply outside the body in a liquid or gel designed to nourish it).
- When the pure culture of the bacterium is injected back into a healthy host, the host must become infected with that specific disease.
- The bacterium must then be isolated from the newly infected host.

Tests done using the spirochete Burgdorfer found inside the ticks met all these conditions and confirmed his expectation: The agent causing Lyme disease had finally been found. In 1983, at the International Symposium of Lyme Disease, the Lyme bacterium was named *Borrelia burgdorferi* in honor of its discoverer.

CHAPTER TWO

THE EFFECTS OF LYME DISEASE

In the past, doctors believed Lyme disease had three separate, easily recognizable stages. Each stage was associated with certain symptoms that were expected to get worse over time if the disease was left untreated. In more recent years, however, experts have recognized that the disease does not always follow predictable time periods and the symptoms do not always follow each other in the same sequence. Due to this, the concept of Lyme having clear-cut, standardized stages has been dropped by many doctors and health organizations. However, some symptoms are more likely to be experienced in the later stages of the disease than immediately after the person has been infected. This can help doctors guess at how long the person has had the disease. Some symptoms do not appear for months or even years after infection occurs. Lyme disease is a multisystemic disease, which means it has symptoms that affect all parts of the body and not all patients experience similar symptoms. This makes diagnosis challenging for patients and doctors who are unfamiliar with Lyme disease.

The First Signs

After a bite from an infected tick, Lyme infection starts in the skin and bloodstream. The

best-known symptom of Lyme disease—a red
rash known as erythema migrans (EM)—generally appears anywhere from 3 to 30 days after the
tick bite. (A rash that occurs immediately after a
tick bite is most likely just a minor allergic reaction to the tick's saliva.) EM begins as a small, red
area that expands over the next several days, sometimes growing to more than 1 foot (30.48 cm) in
diameter if untreated, but often fading on its own
after three to four weeks. This red inflammation
is the result of the immune system beginning to
fight against the foreign bacteria that have been

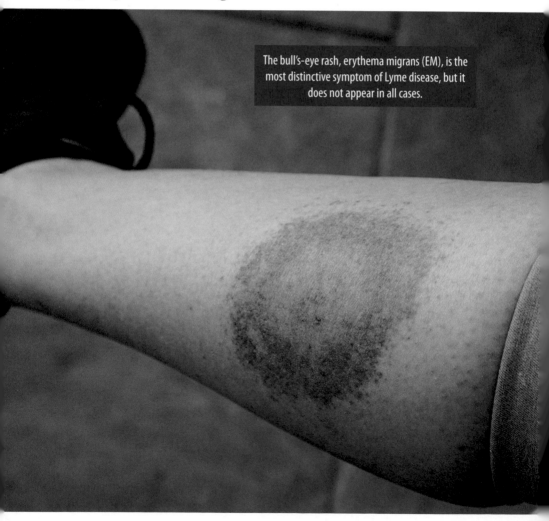

The bull's-eye rash, erythema migrans (EM), is the
most distinctive symptom of Lyme disease, but it
does not appear in all cases.

introduced into the body.

As the spirochetes move away from the site of the bite, the immune reaction and inflammation follow, which in some cases, cause the inner area of the rash to become paler in appearance and develop one or more bright red rings around it, giving it the appearance of a bull's-eye. This rash does not always occur, however, and in some people the rash is not circular in shape at all, but triangular, rectangular, or oval. EM is generally not painful, itchy, or scaly, but it can feel warm to the touch. The most common locations on the body for an EM rash are the armpits, waistline, groin, thighs, stomach, back, and backs of the knees. EM can easily go undetected depending on where it appears on the body. For instance, it is unusual for someone to examine the backs of their own knees on a regular basis, and if they wear pants or long skirts, other people might not see it either.

As with many aspects of Lyme disease, there is disagreement in the medical profession over how many patients with Lyme develop the EM rash. According to the CDC, the figure is 80 percent, but according to the International Lyme and Associated Diseases Society, a nonprofit group of physicians dedicated to the diagnosis and treatment of Lyme disease, less than 50 percent of patients with Lyme recall having a rash. Regardless of the statistical difference, EM is so strongly associated with Lyme that, according to the Infectious Diseases Society of America (IDSA), it is "the only manifestation of Lyme disease in the United States that is sufficiently distinctive enough to allow clinical diagnosis in the absence of laboratory confirmation."[3] In other words, if a doctor observes the EM rash on a patient, no further testing is necessary to prove that the patient has Lyme disease.

Other common symptoms often experienced by people shortly after being bitten can include headaches, dizziness, tingling and numbness, memory and concentration problems, stomach problems, sleepiness, overwhelming joint pain, and fatigue.

The Spreading Infection

If a person infected with Lyme disease does not seek treatment, the disease moves from the bloodstream to organs such as the heart, brain, and joints. When this occurs, the symptoms are varied and affect multiple systems of the body. They may include headaches, a stiff neck, tingling or numbness in the arms and legs, blurred vision, high fever, severe fatigue, enlarged lymph glands, slowing of the heart, pains in the joints and muscles, and facial paralysis.

The facial paralysis that sometimes occurs with Lyme disease is a condition known as Bell's palsy. The inflammation that comes with Lyme infection damages the nerves that control muscles on one side of the face, causing it to droop. The person will have a lopsided smile and may drool or be unable to close the eye on the affected side of the face completely. They may also have pain in or around the ear, lose the ability to taste, or suffer from increased sensitivity to sound. If someone has Bell's palsy along with some or all of the other symptoms listed, it is a major indicator of Lyme disease. Over time, the paralysis often improves without treatment.

Less likely to clear on their own, however, are the joint pains associated with Lyme as it moves through the body. These pains are most often

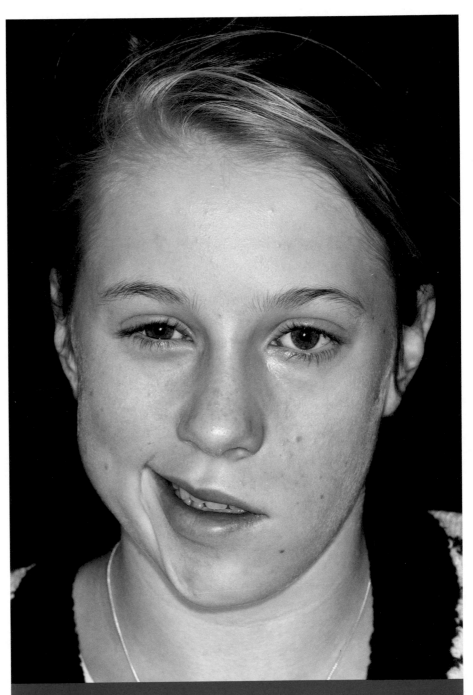

Bell's palsy causes partial facial paralysis, as shown here.
It is generally temporary, but it can be distressing to patients while it lasts.

associated with the larger joints such as the knees, elbows, or shoulders and can shift from one joint to another. The joints and tendons are not always visibly swollen at this point.

Joint pain is a common symptom for Lyme patients.

One Lyme sufferer who experienced advanced symptoms was Jason Weintraub, the son of science journalist Pamela Weintraub, whose entire family also contracted the disease. Pamela described her son's struggle with the infection in her 2008 book, *Cure Unknown: Inside the Lyme Epidemic*:

> Slowly the "flu" went away, but Jason never got well. He now had pain that traveled around his body from joint to joint, constant headache and stomachache, a hacking cough, and inexplicable [unexplained] insomnia and fatigue. His neck

hurt so much that sometimes he could not lift his head from his pillow for days. He dropped from all his sports activities—they were simply too exhausting for him. He stopped doing his homework. He refused to see friends, even his two best friends. On more and more days he could not get up for school.[4]

Lyme Abroad

Lyme disease in Europe is typically caused by two strains of *B. burgdorferi* bacteria named *B. afzelii* and *B. garinii*, although some cases are caused by the primary U.S. strain, *B. burgdorferi* sensu stricto. The process of diagnosis and treatment for European Lyme disease is generally the same as in the United States.

Differences, however, can exist in the symptoms. While most are the same on both continents, European patients can also suffer from borrelial lymphocytoma, which is a bluish-reddish discoloration of the skin that generally occurs on the earlobe, chest, or scrotum (the pouch of skin that contains a man's testicles). It is often, though not always, caused by infection with *B. afzelii*. A second symptom found only in Europe—also affecting the skin and most frequently due to *B. afzelii* infection—is acrodermatitis chronica atrophicans. This condition is a chronic inflammation of the skin, generally on the arms or legs, which, if untreated, can lead to skin atrophy, a condition in which the skin gets thinner.

How Lyme Affects the Nerves

A common symptom of Lyme disease is the appearance of neurological disruptions. When Lyme reaches the central nervous system, it can cause issues such as depression, hallucinations, panic attacks, seizures, and memory problems.

Amy Tan, a best-selling author and Lyme patient, described her symptoms in a 2013 article for the *New York Times*. She wrote, "I could not read a paragraph and recall what it said. I wrote in circles, unable to tie two thoughts together, never mind the plot of a novel."[5]

A frequent neurological symptom of Lyme sufferers is "brain fog," which is characterized by

Author Amy Tan's Lyme disease interfered with her
ability to write, which affected her career.

lapses in memory, extreme fatigue, difficulty sleep-
ing, and an inability to concentrate. A Belgian
man named Chris Le Hérou, speaking during his
ordeal, said,

> I do not see the world the same as before. I do not
> even know any more, when my car is stopped by
> a traffic light, if the light is red or green. I see
> only some of the vehicles I cross, or maybe I see

*them all, but my brain doesn't tell me any more
... And I do not have energy any more. I want
to sleep, sleep, as everything hurts me.*[6]

People with brain fog must sometimes search
for words or names that would normally come
easily to them or have difficulty with simple
motor skills. A Lyme patient may go out to run
an errand and find themselves unable to remember
the route home afterward. According to psychia-
trist Robert Bransfield, "One patient had a panic
attack when they were lost in their garage and
had lost the spatial awareness of the location of
the door."[7]

Loss of sensation in the arms and legs, or a
feeling of "pins and needles," also often occurs in
this stage. In severe undiagnosed cases, symptoms
of late-stage Lyme can resemble those of a stroke,
including severe weakness on one side of the
body. Neurologist John Halperin discovered this
was due to damage done to the body's nerve cells
by the disease. In some Lyme sufferers, however,
depending on the extent of the cellular damage,
the opposite effect can occur, resulting in extreme
sensitivity and pain. One woman recalled,

*It all started with a very bad sore throat. Af-
ter the sore throat continued to persist for more
than a few days my parents took me to the doctor. As many might assume, the doctor said it
was probably something viral and it should
subside in no time. Well, it didn't. My throat
pain continued to progress and now the pain
was accompanied by an excruciating headache.
My headaches were so bad that I was crying
out in pain and holding my head, begging for
it to stop. Also, I was now hurting all over my
body with the most severe pain that I had ever*

*experienced. Something was not right and my
parents knew it.*[8]

People who have Lyme disease, especially these
people with these symptoms, often feel distressed
and frustrated. Because their disease is not visible the way a broken leg is, they may be accused
of faking their symptoms or told things that are
unhelpful, such as, "Just try harder to remember
things," or "You would feel better if you exercised/
ate different food/etc." People with Lyme disease
have different physical and mental limitations
than healthy people, so rather than giving them
unasked-for advice, friends and family members
who want to help their loved one with Lyme disease should be patient and not expect the person
to act the way a healthy person would. They can
also make specific offers of help, such as, "Would
you like a ride to the doctor?" Often, people with
Lyme disease appreciate someone simply offering
their company. Having Lyme disease, like other
chronic invisible illnesses, can make a person feel
isolated because they cannot do all the things they
used to do with their friends, so it is important for
loved ones to reach out and offer to be there for
the person.

Advancing Symptoms

Approximately 60 percent of undiagnosed Lyme
patients develop swelling and pain in one or more
of the joints, which is sometimes referred to as
Lyme arthritis. Frequently, the swelling involves
one of the knees, but many joints can be affected,
including those of the hands or the joint where
the lower jaw connects to the skull.

An advanced and serious complication of Lyme
disease affects the heart. Between 4 and 10 percent

of Lyme disease patients develop heart problems. These can include conduction defects (problems with the electrical pathways and muscle fibers that conduct impulses through the heart), an unusually rapid heart rate accompanied by an irregular rhythm, or inflammation of the heart wall and the sac surrounding it.

A Brief History of Lyme

Although Lyme disease was first seriously studied in the United States in the 1970s, the disease had been previously described by doctors in Europe for almost a century, although experts were often unaware of its causes. For instance, in 1883, a German physician named Alfred Buchwald observed the first reported case of acrodermatitis chronica atrophicans.

In 1909, Swedish doctor Arvid Afzelius presented research he had done on an expanding skin rash that would later come to be known as erythema migrans (EM). In 1921, Afzelius connected the rash with the development of joint pain. He also theorized that ticks transmitted the illness.

Rudolph Scrimenti, a dermatologist (skin doctor), first documented the EM rash in the United States in 1970, five years before Lyme's official "discovery" in Lyme, Connecticut. Scrimenti successfully treated the patient with penicillin, basing his actions on the literature of doctors who had encountered a similar disease.

Finally, Lyme can also affect a person's eyesight. Symptoms in this category can range from mild sensitivity to light and the appearance of "floaters"—small specks in a person's field of vision—to dangerous inflammation of the optic nerve.

A Winding Diagnostic Path

Diagnosing Lyme disease from symptoms alone can be difficult for most of the medical community. Unless a person displays the telltale EM rash, a doctor may not immediately suspect Lyme, especially if the area in which the sick person lives is not an area where Lyme is commonly found. Many doctors in these locations may not recognize the warning signs. In the Lyme documentary *Under Our Skin*, Jordan Fisher Smith of Nevada City, California, recalled his difficulty in obtaining a correct diagnosis:

> *My case was sort of cut and dried. A) I was a park ranger. B) I knew exactly when I was bitten and I saved the tick and brought it to my doctor. C) I had a red rash. And D) I had a rather classic case of neurological Lyme with all the usual trimmings. But I brought all that to the doctors and it took five doctors to figure it out.*[9]

Smith estimates his misdiagnosis cost him between $75,000 and $100,000 in doctors' visits and incorrect medications.

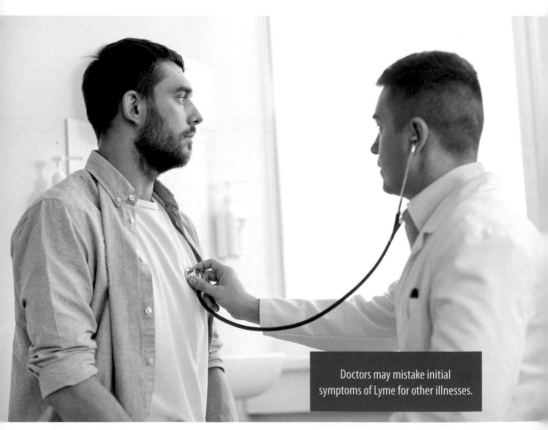

Doctors may mistake initial symptoms of Lyme for other illnesses.

Another difficulty faced by doctors and patients is that the symptoms of Lyme can often resemble those of other illnesses. In the early stage of infection, if no rash is present, Lyme can easily be mistaken for the flu. Acute Lyme symptoms—those that appear suddenly and last a relatively short time—can mimic mononucleosis, a disease that causes extreme fatigue. If undiagnosed Lyme progresses to the early neurological stage, the headache, stiff neck, and fatigue resemble the symptoms of disorders such as viral meningitis, lupus, and multiple sclerosis. Other tick-borne illnesses, such as tick-borne relapsing fever and Rocky Mountain spotted fever, also share many symptoms in common with Lyme disease.

The symptoms of Lyme can be frustrating both in how nonspecific or misleading they can sometimes be and also in the fact that they may disappear and then suddenly reappear. Brian Fallon, director of the Lyme and Tick-Borne Disease Research Center at New York's Columbia University, stated,

> *I think there are a number of general aspects of Lyme disease that cause distress and confusion. One is that symptoms fluctuate. Patients often feel worse on some days, better on others. That confuses parents, school systems, employers, and spouses. It's a difficult aspect of this illness.*[10]

Multiple Infections

Another issue that can complicate many aspects of Lyme disease—from symptoms to diagnosis to treatment—is that of coinfections, which is when multiple infections are present at the same time. Lyme is not the only disease that can be transmitted by ticks.

Two of the most common diseases found in these coinfections are babesiosis and ehrlichiosis. Babesiosis is caused by a parasite called *Babesia microti*, which infects a person's red blood cells. (A parasite is an organism that lives in or on another organism from which it feeds.) Ehrlichiosis, like Lyme, is transmitted by a bacterium. Two types of ehrlichiosis have been

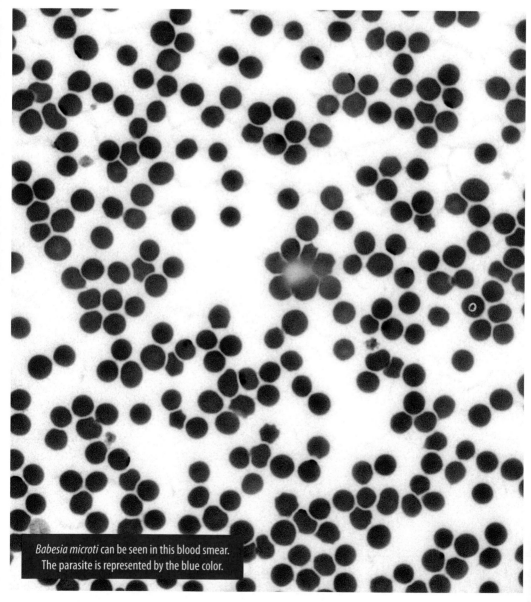

Babesia microti can be seen in this blood smear. The parasite is represented by the blue color.

identified in the United States: human monocytic ehrlichiosis, which is caused by bacteria called *Ehrlichia chaffeensis*, and human granulocytic ehrlichiosis, which is caused by *Anaplasma phagocytophilum*. The terms "monocytic" and "granulocytic" refer to the types of white blood cells in the body that are attacked by the bacteria. Although babesiosis and both types of ehrlichiosis are the most common Lyme coinfections, more might be discovered as research continues.

CHAPTER THREE

TREATING A COMPLEX DISEASE

Getting an accurate diagnosis, although tricky, is the first step toward effectively treating Lyme disease. Doctors can narrow down their options by asking certain common-sense questions. For instance, if the person says they have recently been in a location where Lyme disease is a known threat or if they have been doing an activity that increases their risk of encountering ticks, such as hiking in the woods, the doctor will know not to rule out Lyme disease right away. To see whether the bacteria that cause Lyme disease are present in the patient's body, the doctor may order serological tests, which examine blood serum—the liquid in blood that separates from it when it clots. Instead of testing for the presence of the bacteria, most serological tests are indirect tests, which means they measure the body's reaction to the bacteria. For instance, tests may involve looking at the number of antibodies in the person's blood. Antibodies are specialized proteins created by white blood cells that recognize and target organisms that invade the body—in this case, the *Borrelia* bacteria—and seek to kill them. An organism that causes the body to produce antibodies is called an antigen. If the person has a higher than normal number of antibodies, it is one sign that they may have Lyme disease.

To test for Lyme antibodies, doctors currently use a two-step method consisting of a screening test known as an enzyme-linked immunosorbent assay (ELISA) and a more specific confirmatory test known as a Western blot. These tests, however, can be problematic and are not without their critics among both patients and medical professionals. A great deal of detective work becomes necessary to figure out whether the patient has Lyme or another disease that has similar symptoms. A thorough process of elimination becomes a medical necessity, but this makes the diagnostic process take a long time, which is frustrating to both doctor and patient. This can be exacerbated, or made worse, by the fact that doctors often have many patients to

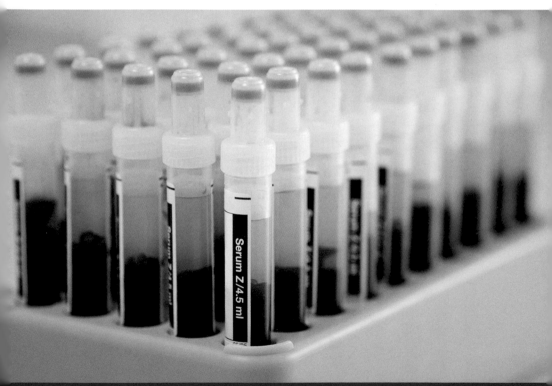

Tests for Lyme disease examine blood serum. In this picture, the yellowish serum can be seen in the top layer of the liquid in the test tube. The red layer on the bottom is a blood clot formed by the rest of the materials in the blood.

see, which can result in short appointments. This may make the patient feel as though not enough time is being devoted to their problem. Both parties must have patience, which becomes difficult when the patient feels the anxiety of uncertainty and doctors have a delicate balancing act with their patients.

ELISA Testing

In the ELISA test, samples of a person's serum are placed into a plastic tray full of numerous wells, or small holes designed to hold liquid. In each well is a tiny amount of dead Lyme bacteria. If antibodies to the bacteria (Antibody A) exist in the blood serum sample, they will stick to the bottom of the well and will remain after the wells are rinsed with purified water. If Antibody A is not present, the serum is completely washed away.

After the wells are rinsed, another solution is added to them. This solution contains antibodies that react to other antibodies (Antibody B); Antibody B sticks to any Antibody A particles that remain after the first rinse. Antibody B has an enzyme linked to it. An enzyme is a protein that can produce certain chemical changes in organic substances. In the case of the ELISA, this enzyme causes dye to change colors.

An hour after Antibody B and its enzyme have been added to the wells, the plastic tray is rinsed out again. The dye is then added to the samples, and if Antibody B is still present, the dye will change color. If this happens, it is a sign to the researchers that Antibody A was present in the original blood sample. The presence of Antibody A in the blood serum indicates that the person being tested has been exposed to the disease. This process needs both steps because the dye will not show up if only Antibody A is present. It takes the reaction of Antibody B to make the sample visible to researchers.

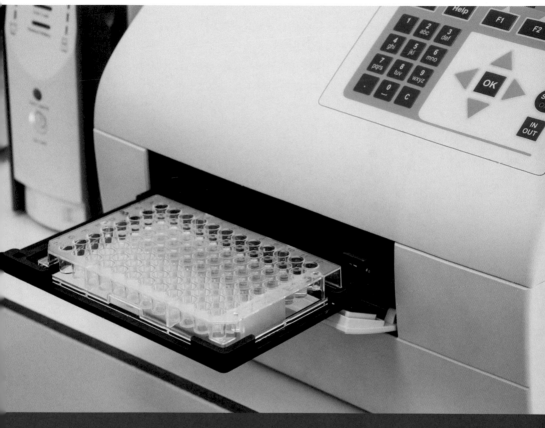

The ELISA test involves putting serum samples and antibodies into a tray full of wells, similar to the one shown here.

Western Blot Testing

According to CDC protocol, if a patient's ELISA comes back positive or if the results are unclear, a Western blot test is then performed. The Western blot is more precise, allowing the laboratory to determine which antigen the antibodies are reacting to. This is useful because other antigens similar to those responsible for Lyme—such as the ones that cause syphilis or mononucleosis—can also bind with the antibodies produced against Lyme. This is known as cross-reacting, and without further testing, someone might receive the wrong diagnosis.

In a Western blot test, *B. burgdorferi* bacteria are put into a detergent that breaks up the proteins from which they are made. These proteins come in different sizes and are electrically charged. The proteins are placed onto a gel that contains many holes and spaces, and an electrical current is applied to the gel. This causes the proteins to move through the gel, with the smaller proteins moving the fastest and reaching the bottom of the gel first. Once the proteins have all been grouped according to size, they are moved from the gel onto a thin sheet and separated into bands. The patient's blood serum is introduced to the proteins on the sheet. If antibodies related to any of the proteins are present in the serum, those antibodies bind to that specific protein band. If none of the antibodies bind to the proteins, it means the person does not have Lyme disease.

The current CDC standard for a Western blot to be positive states that for early-stage infection, antibodies must attach to two out of three specific protein bands. For a person in the later stages of the disease to be considered positive, antibodies must attach to five out of ten bands.

The Testing Debate

Many experts agree that the ELISA and Western blot tests, despite being the way Lyme disease is currently diagnosed, are far from perfect. One basic shortcoming of the ELISA test is that it is less effective in the very early stage of Lyme infection. If a person is given an ELISA test before the body has had a chance to produce antibodies to the bacteria, the ELISA will be negative, even though that person may have Lyme disease. This is especially critical in patients who do not have the telltale EM rash. If a doctor does not see a rash and an ELISA test is negative, a case of Lyme may go undiagnosed.

Another issue is that not all ELISA and Western blot tests are evaluated at the same place. Many different laboratories and hospitals perform the tests, and the degree of accuracy can vary. In an experiment conducted by doctors in the mid-1980s, samples of a patient's blood serum were sent to two separate labs. The serum tested positive for Lyme disease at one and negative at the other. Then, the doctors sent several samples of a single patient's blood serum to labs but labeled the samples as though they were from more than one person. In some cases, the samples were reported as testing positive, while other samples, from the exact same patient and being evaluated at the exact same lab, were reported as testing negative. Interpreting the tests is not always straightforward. Paul Fawcett, a specialist in Lyme blood tests, described the difficulties in interpreting a Western blot:

> *Some of these bands lie within a millimeter [of each other]. You can't be sure that a band you're calling positive is really the correct one. Look at the CAP [College of American Pathologists] surveys ... different labs using the same samples and the same strips are getting different results, showing different bands. The manufactured kits contain a ... test strip that's used [to determine which bands are which]. You can line up the test strip and the strip from the patient and you have to slide them back and forth to properly line them up.*[11]

Critics point out that the CDC's approved band pattern for a positive Western blot test was decided upon using a single strain of B. burgdorferi, when there are hundreds of strains of the bacteria, with protein coats that can vary and cause different bands to be affected.

A second major issue raised by doctors and patients has to do with two protein bands that the scientists who created the Western blot decided to leave off the test. These two proteins, outer surface protein A and outer surface protein B, are "both so specific to the Lyme spirochete that they could come from nothing but exposure to B. burgdorferi and were even candidates for making Lyme vaccines,"[12] according to Weintraub. The reason given for not including these two protein bands was that they were not among the 10 most common bands among patients who tested positive for the disease.

Despite these shortcomings, the CDC says the two-step ELISA and Western blot method is effective in diagnosing Lyme. Experts claim that in later phases of the disease, the ELISA test is about 95 percent sensitive and 95 percent specific. This means that it will give a positive result in 95 percent of people who truly have the disease and a negative result in 95 percent of those who truly do not. Not surprisingly, these statistics are disputed by other experts, who claim the numbers are actually much lower. Scientists at Stony Brook University Medical Center, who have done large amounts of research on Lyme, have suggested that a better way to diagnose the illness might be to run the tests on a patient several times over an extended period of time to look for changes in the results. However, this is rarely done.

Testing Bacterial DNA

Other tests, which are given to patients far less often that serological tests, seek to detect the actual DNA of the *B. burgdorferi* bacteria rather than just antibodies formed against it. These are known as direct tests.

In the early stages of Lyme, if an EM rash is present, the doctor can do a skin culture. A sample of the infected skin is taken and sent to a laboratory, where it is tested for the presence of the bacteria. Placing a sample in a petri dish full of nutrients will encourage bacteria to grow to the point where they will be observable under a microscope. It is important to diagnose Lyme disease quickly to prevent any permanent damage, so skin cultures are not often done because they take longer to show results than indirect tests. Generally, results can take weeks. During this time, the infection may spread further throughout the body, having severe negative effects on the patient.

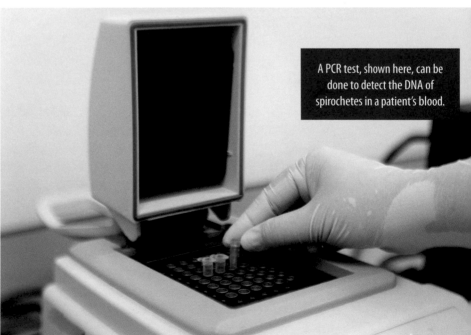

A PCR test, shown here, can be done to detect the DNA of spirochetes in a patient's blood.

The polymerase chain reaction (PCR) test is used for the detection of Lyme in patients who have been undiagnosed for a long time. The PCR blood test is useful for discovering the DNA of spirochetes. If spirochetes are present in the sample, the PCR takes part of the DNA of the bacteria and uses an enzyme to make millions of copies of it, so it is easy to detect using a microscope. PCR tests are an important diagnostic tool for patients with negative ELISA and Western blot results, but the test may need to be conducted multiple times with different bodily fluids to make sure the results are correct.

Prescribing Antibiotics

If it is determined that a person is definitely suffering from Lyme disease, the patient is given antibiotics, which are drugs used to treat infections caused by bacteria. For adults who appear to be in the early stage of the infection, the guidelines set down by the Infectious Diseases Society of America (IDSA) suggest a two- to three-week course (series of doses) of antibiotics. Under the guidelines of the International Lyme and Associated Diseases Society (ILADS), antibiotic treatment may last four to six weeks to make sure all the spirochetes are gone. The specific antibiotics in early stages are taken by mouth, or orally; they include doxycycline (Monodox), amoxicillin (Moxatag), or cefuroxime axetil (Ceftin). In early neurological Lyme, amoxicillin is considered a preferred front-line antibiotic by both ILADS and IDSA, which means it is generally the first thing doctors try because it works well most of the time.

Children under eight years of age can be prescribed amoxicillin or cefuroxime axetil. Doxycycline is avoided for prescriptions for children because

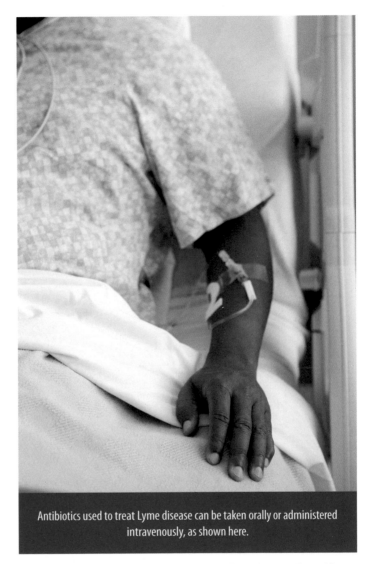

Antibiotics used to treat Lyme disease can be taken orally or administered intravenously, as shown here.

for people under eight years old, it has side effects that can cause permanent yellowing or graying of the teeth or affect a child's growth. Women who are pregnant or breastfeeding should not take doxycycline as it can affect the baby's bone and tooth growth.

In adults and children over eight years old, Lyme arthritis that is not accompanied by any neurological symptoms is typically treated with doxycycline, amoxicillin, or cefuroxime axetil given orally for four weeks. If the joint pain and swelling improve but do not completely clear, another four-week course of oral antibiotics is prescribed. If these symptoms do not improve at all or if they get worse, intravenous (IV) antibiotics are recommended. An IV administers drugs directly into a person's bloodstream, so they act much faster than oral drugs. If the nervous system is also involved, however, the IDSA and ILADS guidelines both suggest the patient be treated with IV antibiotics immediately rather than taking an oral course first. IV antibiotics are also typically given in the advanced stages of Lyme disease.

A person with heart problems caused by Lyme is generally treated with either oral or IV antibiotics for two weeks. Depending on how severe their problems are, they may need to be hospitalized. Patients with advanced heart block (a problem with the heart's electrical system that controls the rate and rhythm of heartbeats) may need to be given a pacemaker, which is a small machine placed under the skin on the chest that helps the heart maintain a more normal rhythm. The pacemaker is removed when the heart problem is fixed.

Alternative Treatment Protocols

Patients who continue to experience symptoms after being treated for Lyme disease may not want to seek further medical treatment or may become unable to due to a lack of money or access to a doctor they feel can correctly address the illness. These patients may turn to alternative treatments in an effort to feel better. Alternative treatments generally do not have clinical studies accepted by the medical establishment that support their effectiveness, and some are even considered dangerous. These treatments can range from fairly

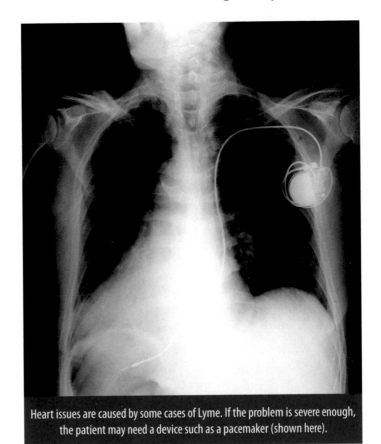

Heart issues are caused by some cases of Lyme. If the problem is severe enough, the patient may need a device such as a pacemaker (shown here).

simple, such as taking mineral supplements, to more complex, such as modern Chinese medicine and herbal treatments.

A well-known figure in the world of herbal medicinal Lyme treatment is Dr. Qingcai Zhang. He treats patients who have been unable to relieve themselves of Lyme symptoms even after years of antibiotic treatments. In 1985, he found that there were Lyme cases in 18 provinces in China. Zhang uses herbs with smaller molecular weight, which is the weight of all the atoms in a chemical compound. Most Western medicinal antibiotics have a dense molecular weight, which makes penetrating the blood-brain barrier (BBB) much more difficult. The BBB is a network of small blood vessels called capillaries that prevents certain materials from moving into the brain from the bloodstream. Crossing the BBB is necessary to treat neurological symptoms.

Herbal naturalist Stephen Buhner created another herbal program that is popular with some chronic Lyme patients. The Buhner protocol is an herbal protocol that, according to his patients, has reduced inflammation, boosted immune system response, and helped the body rid itself of spirochetes. Many doctors who are familiar with Lyme disease have worked with herbal medicine along with traditional Western methods when antibiotic treatment alone has not made symptoms better over a long period of time. Unfortunately, since large amounts of funding are needed for controlled scientific testing, the effectiveness of the herbal protocols is mainly based on patients' stories; not many scientific studies have been done to prove how well they work.

Some Lyme sufferers say they have benefited from treatments in a hyperbaric oxygen chamber. In these sessions, a person sits or lies in the chamber for 30 to 90 minutes and is exposed to air that is 100 percent pure oxygen at higher than normal atmospheric pressure. The air people breathe normally is made up of a combination of gases; along with oxygen, they include nitrogen, argon, and carbon dioxide. Breathing pure oxygen increases blood flow throughout the body and is believed to enhance the performance of the immune system.

Another alternative treatment is a salt and vitamin C protocol, in which a person takes 8 to 16 grams of unprocessed salt and 8 to 16 grams of vitamin C per day. Unprocessed salt is different than traditional table salt—the kind most people have in their salt shaker—because table salt is

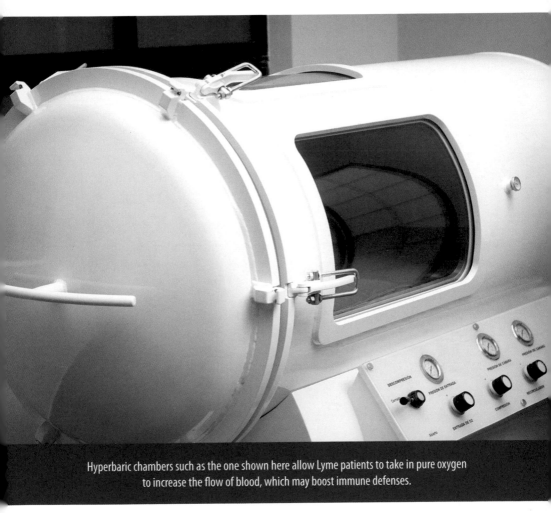

Hyperbaric chambers such as the one shown here allow Lyme patients to take in pure oxygen to increase the flow of blood, which may boost immune defenses.

refined, which means most of the minerals have been removed. Unprocessed salt contains a higher level of minerals that are believed to be helpful to the body. The dosage of each substance starts low and increases over time. According to Bryan Rosner, author of *The Top 10 Lyme Disease Treatments*, this protocol is helpful because salt enhances the effectiveness of a certain enzyme that contributes to white blood cell function and the immune system. He claims that vitamin C, when used with salt, speeds up the healing process and helps remove toxins from the body.

Unprocessed salt (right) is different than common table salt (left).

Unfortunately, some out-of-the-ordinary treatments for Lyme disease have ended with tragic results. John Toth, a physician in Kansas, treated patients with injections of a compound called bismacine, which he was promoting as a cure for Lyme disease. Bismacine had not been studied or proven effective for treating Lyme disease, and worse, it contains high amounts of the metal bismuth and can cause heart and kidney failure. One of Toth's patients, Beverly Wunder, fell into a coma and later died. Toth pleaded guilty to reckless involuntary manslaughter—accidental killing—and spent time in prison. During his trial, Wunder's daughter stated her mother never even had Lyme disease. She stated that "a doctor's greed and disregard for medical regulations and the value of human life cost my mother hers and has

Avoiding Scams

One of the more unusual treatments people have turned to for Lyme disease is the use of rife machines. These machines supposedly work by directing an electromagnetic frequency through the body that breaks apart harmful pathogens. While some people say they can help with Lyme symptoms, others say this improvement may be due to different circumstances such as a change in diet. Many experts say rife machines are useless; their inventor, Royal Raymond Rife, was discredited by the medical community after being unable to scientifically prove his claims that cancer is caused by bacteria that give off different colors and vibrations. His machine, he said, could shatter the bacteria like glass by vibrating at the same frequency as the bacteria. While his ideas gained some notice when they were first introduced in the early 1930s, today, medical experts know that the majority of bacteria do not cause cancer and that it is impossible to destroy them with vibrations from radio waves.

Some people take advantage of ill people searching for a cure; for instance, in 2007, a couple in Washington State were charged with medical fraud:

> They operated a treatment center in their home using a Rife machine among other bogus devices. The man posed as a physician, and his wife scheduled appointments and ... also warned patients not to talk about the treatment they received because it was "unapproved and clandestine [top-secret]."[1]

The couple made thousands of dollars off of patients who were desperately searching for a cure, and at least one patient died of cancer when he chose to use a rife machine as treatment instead of surgery. Distrust of the medical industry can make people with an illness—especially one as difficult to diagnose and treat as Lyme disease—search for creative answers, but it is important for people to research any treatment they come across and discuss it with a licensed doctor before trying it.

1. Andrew Weil, MD, "Ready for Rife?," Dr. Weil, April 30, 2012. www.drweil.com/health-wellness/balanced-living/technology/ready-for-rife/.

forever altered mine."[13] The U.S. Food and Drug Administration (FDA) issued warnings to consumers that bismacine is not an approved drug to treat Lyme disease and is potentially fatal.

CHAPTER FOUR

CHRONIC LYME DISEASE DEBATES

Even after they receive the antibiotic treatment the CDC recommends, 10 to 20 percent of people with Lyme disease do not seem to recover and continue to experience symptoms. Some of these patients, as well as some doctors who treat large numbers of Lyme cases, find that the patients' symptoms do not entirely clear and remain with them chronically, or long-term. This topic has been debated by medical professionals.

Chronic Lyme has been defined as long-lasting or recurring symptoms that begin at the time a person becomes infected with *B. burgdorferi* sensu lato and continue for months or years, even after the standard antibiotic course has been given.

A small group of progressive research doctors from endemic Lyme areas have witnessed their patients' distress. Many of the doctors in this group belong to ILADS. According to the ILADS website,

> *Many patients with chronic Lyme disease require prolonged treatment until the patient is symptom-free. Relapses occur and retreatment may be required. There are no tests currently available to prove that the organism is eradicated [wiped out] or that the patient with chronic Lyme disease is cured.*[14]

These doctors point to studies done on mice, dogs, and most recently, primates. In some of the tested animals, spirochetes were found in bodily fluids even after the proper course of antibiotic treatment had been followed. A 2017 study by researchers at Tulane University found that spirochetes still survived in the organs of the primates after the initial 28-day antibiotic treatment. The lead author of the study, Monica Embers—an assistant professor in microbiology and immunology at the Tulane University School of Medicine—stated that the data within the study shows that the Lyme bacteria can adapt to its host and has the "ability to escape immune recognition, tolerate the antibiotic and invade vital organs such as the brain and heart."[15]

Some doctors, however, including those responsible for creating the IDSA guidelines for treating Lyme, are still unsure whether chronic Lyme exists due to the lack of diagnostic "measureables," such as reliable blood tests for the disease. They argue that many patients show no diagnostic evidence of *B. burgdorferi* spirochetes persisting in the body, therefore they do not recommend prolonged antibiotic treatment to this group of patients regardless of their continuing symptoms.

Most of the IDSA physicians use the term "post-Lyme syndrome" rather than "chronic Lyme" and believe the likely cause of continued symptoms is an autoimmune disruption triggered by the Lyme infection. An autoimmune disease is one that occurs when a person's immune system mistakenly attacks and destroys healthy bodily tissue.

The Detractors

Another reason many doctors do not believe in chronic Lyme disease is because they suspect the symptoms can point to another illness altogether. According to New York Medical College's Raymond Dattwyler, one of the doctors who created the IDSA treatment guidelines, "The majority of people who get the diagnosis of chronic Lyme disease have either depression, fibromyalgia, or another chronic disease ... The tragedy is that sometimes really serious, treatable diseases are ignored."[16]

Lyme Disease in Pop Culture

Several well-known people have been infected with Lyme disease, such as actor Richard Gere, U.S. senator Charles Schumer, and former president George W. Bush. Some celebrities have been outspoken about the disease, which has raised the general public's awareness of it. For instance, Yolanda Hadid, who is the mother of Gigi, Bella, and Anwar Hadid and who has starred on the *Real Housewives of Beverly Hills*, has brought the disease into the public eye by talking frequently about her illness. When several of her castmates questioned whether she was really sick, Hadid said, "That's the most frustrating part of this disease—you look so normal from the outside ... it's a silent killer, an invisible disability that unfortunately is tough."[1] She created a social media campaign to raise awareness; the #LymeDiseaseChallenge encourages people to pose with limes in online photos. Basketball star Elena Delle Donne has also been open about her battle with Lyme, and in 2014, the Lyme Research Alliance named her its first national ambassador. She has been praised as a role model for others with Lyme.

1. Quoted in Grace Gavilanes, "In Her Own Words: How Yolanda Hadid Has Bravely Battled Lyme Disease," *People*, August 23, 2017. people.com/celebrity/yolanda-foster-lyme-disease-battle/diagnosis-doubts/.

Fibromyalgia is a condition that causes chronic, body-wide pain and tenderness in joints, muscles, and tendons. It can also cause extreme fatigue and sleep disorders. Doctors have yet to figure out what causes fibromyalgia. Fibromyalgia has also been controversial in the medical community itself in the past, as diagnosis is based only on signs and symptoms; there are no tests that can be used to confirm a case of fibromyalgia and no drug that can cure it. Physical therapy and counseling are often recommended to treat the symptoms.

Another condition that was once considered

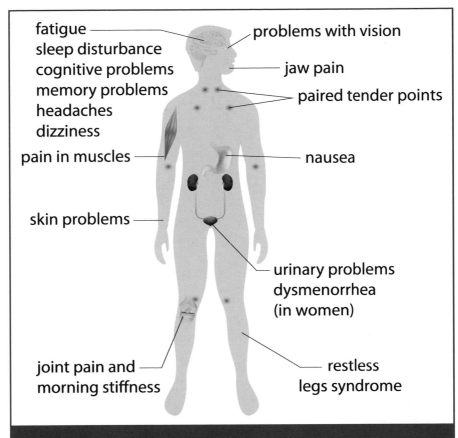

fatigue
sleep disturbance
cognitive problems
memory problems
headaches
dizziness

problems with vision

jaw pain

paired tender points

pain in muscles

nausea

skin problems

urinary problems
dysmenorrhea
(in women)

joint pain and
morning stiffness

restless
legs syndrome

Some of the symptoms of fibromyalgia, described here, are similar to the symptoms of chronic Lyme disease. Some doctors believe chronic Lyme is actually fibromyalgia.

controversial by the medical community but is now much more readily accepted is chronic fatigue syndrome (CFS). This disorder causes extreme fatigue that does not improve with rest and can worsen with physical or mental activity. Some of its other common symptoms resemble those of Lyme: loss of memory or concentration, a sore throat, enlarged lymph nodes, pain that moves from one joint to another, and headache. Like fibromyalgia, the cause of CFS is unknown, and there are no laboratory tests for it or specific medications to treat it.

Depression is perhaps the most controversial disorder that doctors say can be mistaken for chronic Lyme disease. As with fibromyalgia and CFS, some of the symptoms of depression are the same as those experienced by Lyme sufferers, such as slowed thinking, decreased concentration, insomnia, fatigue, and unexplained body aches and pains. It is controversial because some doctors may use depression as a quick and easy diagnosis rather than trying to find the root of the illness. Additionally, this is complicated by the fact that a person with Lyme disease may also have depression at the same time as a result of the uncertainty surrounding their health.

Eugene Shapiro of the Yale Medical Group said he understands why some people prefer a diagnosis of chronic Lyme to an alternative: "They'd rather have Lyme disease than multiple sclerosis. They'd rather have Lyme disease than depression which carries a stigma [a sign of social unacceptability]. They'd rather have Lyme disease than something that nobody can figure out."[17]

Support for Extended Treatment

Some doctors do not like the attitude Shapiro described: that people seek a diagnosis of Lyme disease to feel better about their symptoms. Rafael Stricker, an ILADS officer, said of the patients whose concerns he feels are being dismissed, "The IDSA is basically saying to them, 'We're right, you're wrong, we don't want to listen to you, just take some antidepressants and go away.'"[18]

Doctors such as Stricker are willing to treat patients they believe have chronic Lyme with antibiotics for much longer than is recommended by the IDSA guidelines, and they cite many instances of patients with persistent symptoms who experienced either an improvement or a complete recovery from these symptoms after such treatment. Marie Turley of Tennessee is one such patient. She was bitten by a tick in 1990 and developed symptoms of Lyme shortly after. She failed the laboratory tests for Lyme twice, however, finally receiving a positive Western blot on the third try, a year after the bite occurred. It was only after finding a doctor who agreed to give her antibiotic treatment for more than three years that she felt she had recovered. In her words, "If I had not been fortunate enough … to locate a doctor courageous enough to treat me, I believe that I would either be dead now or crippled, bedridden, and severely mentally ill."[19]

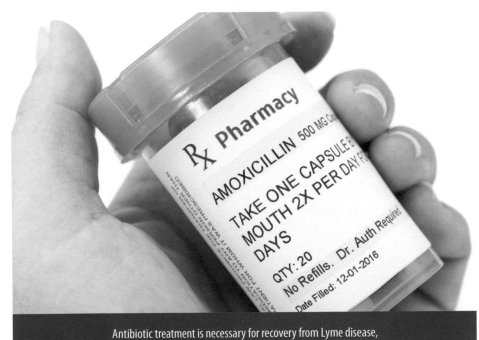

Antibiotic treatment is necessary for recovery from Lyme disease, but just how long a patient should be treated has been a constant debate.

Patients such as Turley thank doctors who were willing to treat them based on patient-centered experience in the clinical diagnosis of Lyme disease. Kenneth Liegner, an ILADS member, said, "When I first started treating, I treated by the book, but it became very clear those regimens weren't working ... it began to dawn on me that the treatment we were giving wasn't treating the infection."[20]

These doctors point to several reasons why Lyme can be such a difficult disease to cure. For one, antibodies work by recognizing the outer protein of an antigen and binding to it. A Lyme bacterium can change its outer protein coat, fooling the antibody into ignoring it. Also, after a person has been infected with Lyme for a longer period of time, the spirochetes move to areas of the body that do not receive much blood flow, which makes it difficult for antibiotics to reach them.

In addition, some scientists believe that spirochetes can escape antibodies as well as antibiotics by actually hiding inside the body's other cells. Another theory is that, if faced with unwelcome conditions, a spirochete can build a cyst around itself with a wall that cannot be penetrated by antibiotics. Meanwhile, repeated and prolonged use of the same antibiotic may become less effective. Patients whose doctors have given them more personalized treatments have reported gradual improvement.

Firm in its belief that extended treatment can be necessary in certain cases, ILADS created its own set of evidence-based guidelines that contradict the IDSA's. These guidelines advocate for the patient's duration of treatment to be based on how their symptoms respond rather than a standardized number of weeks. Many patients seek out doctors who support this treatment method. Unfortunately, these doctors are often located in endemic areas—which can mean a long trip for patients—and have long waiting lists for appointments.

An Unpopular Opinion

Allen Steere, the man credited with discovering Lyme disease in the United States, is a professor of rheumatology at Harvard University. He has written more than 300 articles on Lyme disease and helped write the treatment guidelines recommended by IDSA.

Steere does not believe in the existence of chronic Lyme disease and believes in general that the disease is overdiagnosed and overtreated. He says he sees Lyme as a clear-cut disease, not one that produces a wide variety of vague symptoms, as some doctors believe.

Steere's position has made him an unpopular man among those in the Lyme community who have dealt with persistent symptoms of Lyme disease. People have protested his speaking engagements, and he has been threatened on several occasions, although he does have people who support him and his view of the disease.

Taking a Risk

Long-term antibiotic treatment may improve Lyme symptoms, but it is not without risks. In addition to targeting pathogens, antibiotics can also kill useful bacteria that live in the human digestive system. This can lead to yeast infections, which are fungal infections that affect the genitals, skin, or mouth. Antibiotics can also cause an inflammation of the bowels known as colitis, the symptoms of which include abdominal pain and bloody diarrhea.

Other problems can arise when people receive IV medication. Patients on long-term IV therapy often have a special line called a peripherally inserted central catheter (PICC) line inserted beneath the skin. This line leads into a large vein in the chest, near the heart, and the medication is delivered through the line into the vein. The presence of the line may cause blood clots in the body, and infections may also occur. According to Jonathan Edlow, one woman died from "massive fungal infection caused by an intravenous catheter that had been in place for more than two years so she could receive ceftriaxone for Lyme disease."[21]

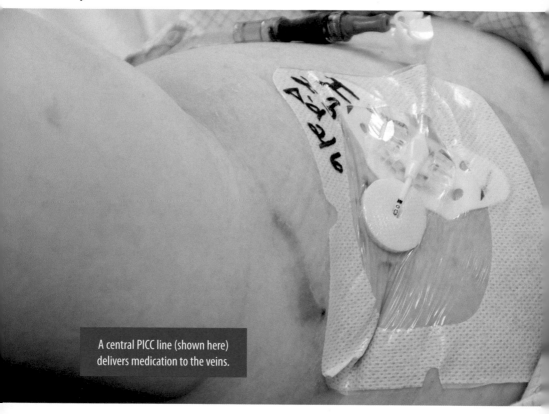

A central PICC line (shown here) delivers medication to the veins.

Another concern that has been very prominent in the media in recent years is a fear that the overuse of antibiotics can lead to drug-resistant bacteria. Whenever a person takes an antibiotic, while many pathogens are destroyed, a few will resist the antibiotic and survive. These surviving bacteria can then multiply, passing on their antibiotic resistance to the new bacteria that are created. Thus, the next time an antibiotic is prescribed to cure an illness caused by that bacteria, it will be much less effective. Also, weaker bacteria can acquire genetic material from other antibiotic-resistant bacteria near them through various methods of transmission, which results in the weaker bacteria becoming antibiotic-resistant as well. If bacteria become antibiotic-resistant, even the current treatments will no longer work.

Opposition to Extended Treatment

In addition to these worries about the medical complications that can develop from an overuse of antibiotics, doctors who do not believe in chronic Lyme state other reasons why they believe long-term treatment is not a logical solution. In cases where patients report improvement in their symptoms after extended antibiotic treatment, the IDSA said this could be due to one of three reasons: The patient has a strong mental belief that the treatment will help, so they feel like their symptoms have improved—a situation that is known as the placebo effect; antibiotics do help reduce inflammation in many cases, which can lead to an improvement in some symptoms; or the person had another illness besides Lyme that responded positively to the antibiotics. These doctors point to clinical trials that they say prove no benefit to prolonged treatment, although ILADS members have argued that these trials had serious design flaws and that one of them was even halted halfway through.

Critics of long-term treatment also point to the cost to patients. According to Phillip Baker, one of the doctors involved with three Lyme clinical trials, extended therapy can cost a person as much as $50,000 per year. He believes doctors who advocate for this treatment may be taking advantage of patients. According to him, "the net result is that people are paying a lot of money for something that's not doing them much good."[22]

Caught in the middle of the debate are the patients, who often find themselves confused and untreated. They have their trust in the medical community damaged, and they may not know whom to trust with their health. Brian Ebner of Madison, Wisconsin, was ill for 11 years and saw 24 doctors before finally visiting one who diagnosed him with Lyme. The doctor prescribed long-term treatment that included Ebner taking 106 pills a day. Despite following the doctor's instructions, Ebner had his

Rising costs for standard and alternative therapies can be a heavy burden on a Lyme patient financially as well as emotionally.

doubts. He said,

> *It's hard to figure out what's going on ... It's just crushing. On the one hand you've got your traditional family doctor who says all you need is one month of antibiotics and you're done, and on the other end of the spectrum you have these Lyme-literate persons throwing everything against the wall to see what sticks.*[23]

Legal Battles

Several Lyme-literate doctors have been investigated by state medical boards after being accused of misdiagnosing patients with Lyme disease, causing them harm through treatment procedures, or failing to uphold certain standards of care.

One of the more well-known accused is Dr. Charles Ray Jones from Connecticut, an expert on pediatric Lyme disease. In 2010, the 81-year-old Jones was accused of prescribing medication for a child he had not met and ordering blood and urine tests for patients before seeing them, among other things. Jones defended himself by saying that he only continued a prescription for the child of a nurse he knew well and trusted, and that he ordered the blood and urine tests in advance because he had a six-month wait time to see new patients. After paying a fine and agreeing to have someone monitor his practice, Jones was put on probation but allowed to keep his license.

The other side of the Lyme dispute has been struck by legal blows as well. In 2006, Connecticut attorney general Richard Blumenthal launched an investigation of the IDSA panel that created the Lyme treatment guidelines. One of the more serious accusations Blumenthal made was that certain doctors on the panel were also paid consultants for insurance companies. This could be considered a serious conflict of interest because if the IDSA did recommend long-term antibiotic treatment for Lyme disease, insurance companies would likely be required to pay for it. Thus, from a financial standpoint, it would make sense that these companies would not want the IDSA to advise long-term treatment and might pressure their consultants on the guidelines panel to speak against it. A spokesperson for the IDSA, however, denied that any of the panel members benefited financially from the content of the guidelines.

In 2008, Blumenthal and the IDSA agreed to a review of the guidelines by a new panel, and ultimately the guidelines were upheld. The review

Legislation has broadened a patient's right to choose their treatment for Lyme. Both sides have fought each other in court regarding treatment methods.

panel's report, issued in 2010, stated, "The risk/ benefit ratio from prolonged antibiotic therapy strongly discourages prolonged antibiotic courses for Lyme disease ... Only high-quality, prospective, controlled clinical trial data demonstrating both benefit and safety will be sufficient to change the current recommendations."[24] This ruling caused much anger and dismay in the Lyme-literate community. Pat Smith, president of the nonprofit Lyme Disease Association, issued a statement that criticized the review panel:

> *They admit to receiving a large volume of case reports and case series that attested to "perceived" clinical improvement with long term treatment. One would assume in most cases, doctors were perceiving the improvement in patients and thus their years of clinical judgment would carry significant weight. Yet they excluded all of that evidence as not justified.*[25]

Believers in chronic Lyme have won some important legal support, however. In 2010, a state law was passed in Massachusetts providing protection to doctors who prescribe long-term antibiotic treatment to Lyme patients. In 2015, New York passed legislation protecting doctors as well. Connecticut, Rhode Island, and California have similar laws. M. Jodi Rell, the governor of Connecticut at the time of that state's passage of the Lyme disease bill, issued a press release, stating,

> *Doctors in Connecticut—the absolute epicenter of Lyme disease—can continue to do what is best for their patients suffering from this complex illness ... The bill also recognizes that Lyme disease patients must have the freedom to choose what remedy or regimen best meets their needs.*[26]

It seems unlikely that the uproar over chronic

Lyme will fade any time in the near future, and more legal battles are sure to arise. Until a test is developed that can identify without a doubt the presence of *B. burgdorferi* bacteria in a person claiming to have chronic Lyme, the controversy over its existence and how—or even if—to treat it will continue. "It's like two people speaking different languages and trying to communicate,"[27] said Kenneth Liegner of ILADS, referring to the two sides of the debate.

CHAPTER FIVE

LYME PREVENTION AND FUTURE CONSIDERATIONS

Because diagnosing and treating Lyme disease is so difficult, many experts recommend that people take steps to prevent getting the disease in the first place. Fortunately, there are some simple precautions people can take when they know they will be in an area where ticks are a risk. Additionally, there are some measures state and local governments can take to reduce the number of ticks in an area.

Reducing the Deer Population

Many Lyme experts believe reducing the number of ticks in a particular area can greatly lower the risk of people getting infected. Some communities have attempted to do this by reducing the number of deer in the region. This can be successful because adult deer in urban environments tend to stay within their own home range and do not migrate into areas where deer have been removed. Hiring licensed sharpshooters, holding controlled hunts, and allowing regulated hunting can all contribute to deer reduction.

According to the Connecticut Department of Public Health, controlled hunts carried out between 1996 and 2004 in Groton, Connecticut, made a significant difference in the incidence of Lyme disease. The deer population was reduced from 77 deer per square mile (2.59 sq km) to

10 per square mile after only two years of controlled hunting, and further hunting kept the population at that low level. Reducing the deer population resulted in an 83 percent reduction in Lyme disease incidents among residents.

Local governments have used deer reduction methods to lower the number of deer that remain in populated areas.

Other methods of deer reduction that do not involve killing the deer have been researched but found to be less effective. One approach involved fertility control, in which deer would be shot with a dart containing a birth control agent. This method was found to be effective only in isolated deer populations and was very expensive.

One small-scale practice that has had some success is fencing, which involves putting up fences to keep deer out of particular areas. This is only suitable for a very restricted area, such as an individual's house and yard. Ultrasonic devices are also now available; these detect motion and produce sound waves that deer find unpleasant to listen to.

Getting Rid of Ticks

Other attempts to reduce the number of ticks in a particular area focus on killing the ticks themselves. One method recommended by the ALDF is the four-poster bait station. The bait station has a central bin filled with corn and a feeding station at either end. When deer eat the corn, their ears rub against rollers mounted on the feeding stations. These rollers are coated in pesticide that kills any ticks attached to the deer's ears, head, neck, and shoulders. As the deer grooms itself, it spreads pesticide onto other parts of its body as well. A similar bait station has been developed that places a collar treated with tick pesticide around the deer's neck as it feeds.

Another option is a system that targets the ticks that feed on mice, which are a primary carrier of Lyme disease. Special "tick tubes," which contain cotton that has been treated with a pesticide that kills ticks, are placed in areas mice visit a lot. Mice take this cotton to build their nests, and the pesticide helps eliminate ticks in their larval and nymphal stages while leaving the mice unharmed.

Some people treat their yards with pesticides to reduce the tick population. It is recommended that pesticide spray be applied once in the late spring or early summer to control tick nymphs, with a second application in October to target adult ticks. The pesticide should be sprayed on tick habitat areas only, such as ground cover shrubs near the house or walkways and areas where the lawn meets the woods. Several yards beyond the woodland border should also be treated, as this is where a high concentration of ticks can generally be found.

Individual Actions

There are also steps individuals can take to protect themselves against ticks when walking or playing outdoors. While it is best to stay clear of tick-infested areas altogether, this simply may not be possible for everyone. People should avoid contact with leaf litter and overgrown vegetation and walk in the center of woodland trails.

Clothing should be light in color so any ticks that attach to it will be easily visible. Long pants, long-sleeved shirts, and hats are recommended, and long hair should be tied back. Pants may be tucked into socks and shirts tucked into pants to provide fewer entry points for ticks to reach the skin. Shoes that cover the entire foot should always be worn in areas that are known to contain ticks.

A person can also use insect repellent. One that contains 20 percent DEET (the most common active ingredient in such repellents) can be applied to bare skin as well as clothing. DEET works by turning off receptors on the tick's antennae that it uses to detect the presence of a human. Because DEET is a powerful toxin, it should not be applied near the eyes or nose, to broken skin, or to skin that is covered by clothing after the spray is applied. Users should also be careful not to inhale DEET.

Using insect spray and limiting ticks' access to skin—such as by tucking pants into socks, as shown here—are two helpful actions that can be taken when walking in the woods.

Another chemical called permethrin, which kills ticks on contact, can be applied to clothing but not to skin.

Upon returning from a tick-infested area, a person should do a thorough check for ticks, using a mirror to examine hard-to-see areas such as the armpits, scalp, backs of the knees, and groin. Clothing should be checked before entering the home and then washed in hot water and dried on high heat for at least 30 minutes.

If an attached tick is found on a person, certain steps should be taken to ensure its safe removal. Using fine-tipped tweezers, grab the tick as close to the skin as possible. Gentle pressure should then be used to pull the tick straight up from the skin, without any twisting, jerking, or crushing of the tick's body. Commercial tools specifically designed for removing ticks are also available, and a study of three such tools conducted at The Ohio State University showed them to be more effective at removing tick nymphs than regular tweezers. The hands should be washed immediately after removing the tick, and the site of the bite should be cleaned with an antiseptic. Methods such as applying petroleum jelly (Vaseline) or nail polish to the tick or burning it with a match should not be attempted, as they can cause the tick to discharge saliva—and therefore possibly bacteria—into the skin. Applying a hot match to the tick carries the added risk of burning the person's skin. After removing the tick, the person should then monitor the site of the bite for a rash and notify a doctor if one appears, or if fever, headache, and fatigue occur.

Attempts at a Vaccine

Precautions such as these will be necessary until science can discover a better way to protect the

The Problem of Cost

Antibiotics are the only approved treatment for Lyme disease, so although people report getting relief from other methods, cost is an issue for some people because health insurance companies generally only cover approved treatments. For example, ABC News in Harrisburg, Pennsylvania, reported that although hyperbaric oxygen therapy—which costs $1,000 per week in Pennsylvania's Lancaster County—has had positive outcomes for many patients, it is not covered by insurance because it is considered experimental. According to Julia Wagner of the group Pennsylvania Lyme, "Somebody has to do a study and it has to be rigorous and they have to prove that it actually does have positive outcomes."[1] Until that time, patients generally have to pay out of pocket for treatments other than antibiotics.

1. Quoted in Flora Posteraro, "Why Oxygen Therapy for Lyme Disease Is Not Covered by Insurance," ABC 27 News, January 29, 2018. abc27.com/2018/01/29/why-oxygen-therapy-for-lyme-disease-is-not-covered-by-insurance/.

population against Lyme disease, such as development of a vaccine. A vaccine is a preparation of living or dead microorganisms injected into the body that causes the immune system to act against that particular microorganism. The person does not get sick from this injection because the microorganisms are either dead or too weak to cause any harm, but their presence still provokes the production of antibodies against them. Then, the next time a person is exposed to that microorganism, the body will already have antibodies stored against it, and the illness will be wiped out before the person feels any effects from it.

Although there is no Lyme vaccine available for humans as of 2018, one was briefly on the market. The three-dose vaccine was called LYMErix, and a company called SmithKlein Beecham produced it. The FDA approved LYMErix in 1998, but by 2000, federal health authorities were investigating claims that it was causing severe cases of arthritis in some people and possibly causing old, previously treated infections of Lyme to flare up again in others. Allen Steere, who directed SmithKlein Beecham's trials of the vaccine, said that even though he recommended its passage, the vaccine had the potential to cause an autoimmune reaction in persons with a certain genetic marker, and this reaction could result in treatment-resistant arthritis. The FDA approved the vaccine anyway, and, even after the claims that it was making people sick began rolling in, left it on the market while it attempted to determine if the vaccine was indeed the cause of the problems. Eventually, the FDA stated it could find no compelling evidence LYMErix was unsafe. However, after 121 people filed a lawsuit against the company in 1999, accusing the company of covering up the vaccine's harmful effects, SmithKlein Beecham stopped producing the drug.

The vaccine was created using one of the Lyme bacteria's outer proteins—outer surface protein A—to provoke the body's immune response. Since LYMErix's failure, scientists have been seeking other ways to use this protein without the unfortunate side effects that were reported with LYMErix. Another protein, outer surface protein C, is also being examined as a possible candidate for developing a new vaccine.

Other approaches are being researched as well. Scientists at Yale University are studying the possibility of creating a vaccine that would target the tick itself as it feeds on a vaccinated person. They discovered that a protein present in tick saliva called tick histamine release factor was helping to transmit *B. burgdorferi* from tick to person. Studies done in mice so far have shown that blocking this protein cuts down on the efficiency of the tick's feeding and has resulted in fewer Lyme spirochetes being transmitted to the mice.

Researchers at the CDC have been focusing on a gene activated by the Lyme bacteria during tick feeding that is necessary to transmit infection. They altered the bacteria to disable this gene and then injected the altered bacteria into mice and allowed ticks to feed on them. Next, they took 15 healthy mice and allowed the ticks that had fed on the infected mice to feed on the healthy mice. Only 2 of the 15 mice contracted Lyme, which shows that disabling that particular gene in the bacteria dramatically reduces its ability to move from host to host. The researchers hope to use the knowledge learned from this and other experiments involving this gene to develop a Lyme vaccine.

New research has also found that other types of *Borrelia* bacteria—aside from *B. burgdorferi*—may cause Lyme disease. In these cases, they say, the symptoms may be different; for instance, *B. mayonii* may cause vomiting and a spotty rash rather than the classic EM bull's-eye rash. This would further complicate the already difficult Lyme diagnosis process. However, the researchers acknowledge that it is very rare for these other bacteria to cause Lyme—they say only six Americans have contracted Lyme disease from *B. mayonii* since 2012—and some experts say it is incorrect altogether. More studies must be done to confirm these findings.

New Discoveries

Scientists continue to search for more reliable serological tests to make the diagnosis of Lyme more accurate. One such effort, the C6 ELISA, was developed by researchers at Tulane University and is said by some experts to be highly effective

Animals with Lyme Disease

Lyme disease can affect animals as well as humans, so people should be aware of the signs of Lyme in their pets. Dogs are most commonly the victims of the illness, although cats and other domesticated animals such as horses and cattle can also become infected. Symptoms in dogs and cats commonly include fever, swelling in the joints, difficulty walking, appetite loss, swollen lymph nodes, and unusual drowsiness. Pets do not display the EM rash. If the disease is untreated, serious kidney problems can develop. A blood test may be used to diagnose the illness, but these are often unreliable, so many veterinarians will choose to go by the symptoms along with the animal's history and whether or not the area in which the animal lives has many cases of Lyme. Lyme in pets is treated with antibiotics.

Although there are vaccines against Lyme available for cats and dogs, many veterinarians do not believe they are very effective and do not recommend them. Tick control is important, and putting chemicals that kill insects on pets' skin is a common method of preventing bites. Avoiding taking pets to areas with large numbers of ticks and checking pets for ticks frequently are actions that are also highly recommended.

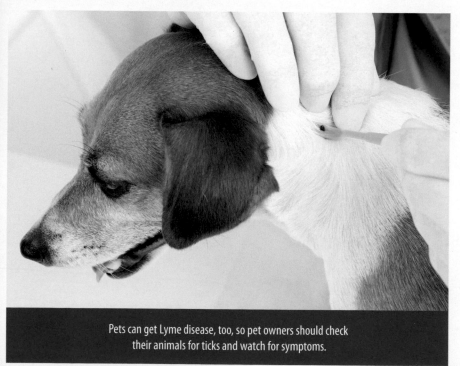

Pets can get Lyme disease, too, so pet owners should check their animals for ticks and watch for symptoms.

in detecting Lyme in its early stages, when the traditional two-tier ELISA/Western blot process can often fail. The C6 ELISA detects antibodies to the C6 peptide found in *B. burgdorferi*. (A peptide is a compound made up of two or more amino acids, which are the building blocks of proteins.) According to Mario Philipp of Tulane,

> *The C6 peptide is part of a lipoprotein, VlsE, which sits on the surface membrane of the spirochete. Parts of this protein are changed by the spirochete as it infects the host, but other portions, C6 included, stay constant and stimulate an early and strong antibody response. This is why the C6 test is so sensitive, as it detects antibody very early in the infection.*[28]

The C6 ELISA can also detect European as well as North American strains of *B. burgdorferi*. Some support exists for the C6 ELISA as a stand-alone test to replace the ELISA/Western blot combination, but other scientists worry about the number of false positives the test can produce. They say more research is needed.

Also being studied for usefulness in diagnosing Lyme is the luciferase immunoprecipitation system (LIPS) test. This type of test has been used to detect viral and fungal infections for a few years, but only recently have scientists begun to try to detect antibody responses to Lyme bacteria with it. In June 2010, Lyme researchers at the NIH reported impressive results using LIPS and expressed the opinion that those results marked LIPS as an efficient method of evaluating antibody responses in Lyme patients.

Further progress in better understanding Lyme was made in 2010 when researchers at the Stony Brook University Medical Center in New York successfully mapped the genetic blueprint of

13 strains of Lyme-causing bacteria. This work could potentially impact all aspects of how the disease is handled. Benjamin Luft, the study's senior author, stated, "By characterizing every gene in the Lyme disease agents family, we have a blueprint of every possible characteristic of the organism. This is the building block to developing more accurate and effective diagnostic tests, therapeutic agents and vaccines."[29]

In addition to new detection methods, new treatments are being researched. Recently, stem cell therapy has been used to treat damage to the body that comes from long-term symptoms. A stem cell is a type of cell that has the potential to turn into any other kind of cell, so stem cells can be inserted into the body where needed. For instance, if a person's nerve cells are damaged, stem cells can become new nerve cells. One recent case study found that stem cell therapy improved muscle strength, mental awareness, coordination, and stamina in a patient with Lyme disease. This was proven with tests, such as magnetic resonance imaging (MRI), that let doctors see changes in a person's nervous system.

A case study is different than a clinical study because it focuses on one person rather than many people. This can be useful to get a general idea of how a treatment might work, but the results should be viewed with caution because each person is different; just because stem cells work for one person does not mean they will work for everyone with the disease. However, it is an important step forward, and others, such as television star Yolanda Hadid, have tried the treatment. Further research is necessary to see how well it works on the general population.

Research in the field of Lyme disease is constantly evolving. Patients are becoming a large

Key Researchers in Lyme

A major force toward understanding Lyme disease is focused research. The Lyme Disease Clinical Research Center at Johns Hopkins University is the first Lyme disease research center in a major department of medicine in the United States. The center applies its focus on the entire spectrum of illness related to Lyme and associated diseases, including problems that appear as the disease moves into the late stages, such as arthritis and post-treatment Lyme disease syndrome.

Dr. John Aucott took the position of director of the Johns Hopkins Lyme Disease Clinical Research Center in April 2015 and is an associate professor of medicine at the Johns Hopkins University School of Medicine. He has been involved in care of patients and research in Lyme disease since joining the Johns Hopkins faculty in 1996.

The father of modern patient-centered Lyme protocols is Dr. Joseph Burrascano. In 2008, he published the pioneering clinical observation *Advanced Topics in Lyme Disease: Diagnostic Hints and Treatment Guidelines for Lyme and Other Tick Borne Illnesses*. This publication, which was created over the course of 24 years of clinical care of Lyme patients, is the basis for the ILADS standard of care for patients with undiagnosed, late-stage Lyme disease. Burrascano stated, "The management of tick-borne illnesses in any given patient must be approached on an individual basis using the practitioner's best judgment."[1]

Burrascano defined three criteria that must exist to diagnose chronic Lyme:

- The illness must be present for at least one year.

- The patient must have persistent major neurologic problems or active joint problems.

- The infection must still be active, meaning the person tests positive for *B. burgdorferi*.

1. Joseph J. Burrascano, *Advanced Topics in Lyme Disease: Diagnostic Hints and Treatment Guidelines for Lyme and Other Tick Borne Illnesses*, 16th edition, October 2008, p. 1. www.lymenet.org/BurrGuide200810.pdf.

and ever-present voice, becoming their own advocates when they feel they are being ignored by the established, standardized medical community. Lyme sufferers, through all of their symptoms and discomforts, have made political and medical strides to take ownership of their own standard of care. For example, in January 2018, Pat Smith of the Lyme Disease Association was able to get a spot on a group that has the power to recommend changes they think Congress should make to federal Lyme disease policy. Smith said, "This could be really significant ... It's the first time we have had patients' voices at the table, and advocates and treating physicians."[30] Practitioners are also being protected in an effort to use emerging studies on treatment outcomes to give their patients a protocol that may help them get better faster. Joseph Jemsek, a physician in Washington, D.C., who specializes in treating Lyme patients, is optimistic about the future:

> *What I sense is that we're at the beginning of something that is going to be huge, just like I had that feeling twenty-some years ago with HIV ... It's going to be an explosive area of medicine and we're going to learn a lot about chronic illness, and I think that's going to help health care tremendously.*[31]

NOTES

Introduction:
"Removing the Nails"

1. Richard I. Horowitz, *Why Can't I Get Better?: Solving the Mystery of Lyme and Chronic Disease.* New York, NY: St. Martin's Press, 2013, p. 84.

Chapter One:
Understanding Lyme Disease

2. Alan G. Barbour, *Lyme Disease: The Cause, the Cure, the Controversy.* Baltimore, MD: Johns Hopkins University Press, 1996, p. 39.

Chapter Two:
The Effects of Lyme Disease

3. Quoted in Constance Bean, *Beating Lyme: Understanding and Treating This Often Complex and Misdiagnosed Disease.* New York, NY: American Management Association, 2008, p. 74.

4. Quoted in Pamela Weintraub, *Cure Unknown: Inside the Lyme Epidemic.* New York, NY: St. Martin's Press, 2008, p. 30.

5. Amy Tan, "My Plight with Lyme Disease," *New York Times*, August 11, 2013. www.nytimes.com/roomfordebate/2013/08/11/deconstructing-lyme-disease/my-plight-with-lyme-disease.

6. Quoted in P.J. Langhoff, *It's All in Your Head: Around the World in 80 Lyme Patient Stories.* Hustisford, WI: Allegory, 2007, p. 222.

7. Robert Bransfield, "The Neuropsychiatric Assessment of Lyme Disease," Mental Health and Illness, accessed January 25, 2018. www.mentalhealthandillness.com/tnaold.html.

8. "Shelby A.," Bay Area Lyme Foundation, accessed January 25, 2018. www.bayarealyme.org/blog/story/shelby-a/.

9. *Under Our Skin*, directed by Andy Abrams Wilson. Sausalito, CA: Open Eye Pictures, 2009, DVD.

10. Quoted in Bean, *Beating Lyme*, p. 74.

Chapter Three:
Treating A Complex Disease

11. Quoted in Jonathan A. Edlow, *Bull's Eye: Unraveling the Medical Mystery of Lyme.* New Haven, CT: Yale University Press, 2003, pp. 177–178.

12. Weintraub, *Cure Unknown*, p. 200.

13. Quoted in Patricia Callahan and Trine Tsouderos, "Some Chronic Lyme Disease Promoters Run Afoul of the Law," *Los Angeles Times*, December 27, 2010. www.latimes.com/health/la-he-lyme-disease-side-2010122706632899.

Chapter Four:
Chronic Lyme Disease Debates

14. "Basic Information About Lyme Disease," International Lyme and Associated Diseases

Society, accessed January 25, 2018. www.ilads. org/lyme/about-lyme.php.

15. Quoted in Maria Clark, "Lyme Disease Can Persist Even After Treatment, Tulane Study Finds," *Times-Picayune*, December 14, 2017. www.nola.com/health/index.ssf/2017/12/ lyme_disease_can_persist_even.html.

16. Quoted in Frederik Joelving, "Few Docs Recognize 'Chronic' Lyme Disease," Reuters, October 22, 2010. www.nlm.nih.gov/medlineplus/ news/fullstory_104718.html.

17. Quoted in Bean, *Beating Lyme,* p. 132.

18. Quoted in Mary Carmichael, "Doctors Debate over Lyme Disease," *Newsweek*, August 6, 2007. www.newsweek.com/2007/08/05/the-great-lyme-debate.html.

19. Quoted in "Faces of Lyme Disease," Lyme Disease Foundation. www.lyme.org/turley.html.

20. Quoted in Amanda Korman, "Two Sides of a Disease," International Lyme and Associated Diseases Society, October 10, 2010. www.ilads. org/news/lyme_news/80.html.

21. Edlow, *Bull's Eye*, p. 213.

22. Quoted in Claudia Kalb, "Lyme Time in D.C: Unraveling How to Best Treat the Disease," *Newsweek*, July 30, 2009. www.newsweek.com/ blogs/the-human-condition/2009.

23. Quoted in Shawn Doherty, "Dispute Spreads on How to Treat Lyme," *Madison (WI) Capital Times*, June 30, 2010. host.madison.com/ct/ news/local/health_med_fit/article_57d2f978-83c2-11df-bf04-001cc4c002e0.html.

24. "Final Report of the Lyme Disease Review Panel of the Infectious Diseases Society of America

(IDSA)," Infectious Diseases Society of America. www.idsociety.org/Content.aspx?id=16520.

25. Pat Smith, "Statement of the National Non Profit Lyme Disease Association, Inc. on the IDSA Guidelines Panel Decision 4-22-10," April 23, 2010. www.lymediseaseassociation. org/index.php?option=com_content&view= article&id=616:idsa-guidelines-panel-decision-4-22-10&catid=7:conflict-report&Itemid=398.

26. "Governor Rell Signs Bill That Shields Doctors in Treatment of Lyme Disease," CT.gov, June 22, 2009. www.ct.gov/governorrell/cwp/view.asp?A=3675&Q=442100.

27. Quoted in Gary Santaniello, "Lyme Disease Divide," *Hartford Courant*, September 17, 2006. articles.courant. com/2006-09-17/features/0609150349_ 1_lyme-disease-corkscrew-shaped-bacterium-lyme-bacterium.

Chapter Five:
Lyme Prevention and Future Considerations

28. Quoted in Denise Lang, *Coping with Lyme Disease: A Practical Guide to Dealing with Diagnosis and Treatment*. New York: Holt, 2004, pp. 58–59.

29. "Genetic Blueprint of Bacteria Causing Lyme Disease Unraveled," Stony Brook University Physicians, October 13, 2010. www. stonybrookphysicians.com/html_community/ news_view.asp?item=31.

30. Quoted in Jerry Carino, "A Golden Opportunity for Change on Chronic Lyme

Disease," *USA Today*, January 9, 2018. www.app.com/story/news/health/2018/01/09/golden-opportunity-change-chronic-lyme-disease/1011461001/.

31. Quoted in Wilson, *Under Our Skin*.

GLOSSARY

antibody: Any of a large number of proteins produced by specialized white blood cells in response to the appearance of an antigen that act against that antigen in an immune response.

antigen: Any substance foreign to the body that causes an immune response.

bacteria: Extremely small single-celled organisms. Many kinds of bacteria are harmless, but some can cause disease.

chronic: Long-lasting or recurrent (coming and going).

endemic: Constantly present to a greater degree in one area than in others.

fatigue: Physical or mental weariness.

immune response: The body's response to an antigen that occurs when white blood cells identify the antigen as foreign and begin the formation of antibodies and other cells that can react with the antigen and make it harmless.

inflammation: A way in which the body reacts to infection, generally characterized by redness, swelling, warmth, and pain.

insomnia: An inability to sleep.

Lyme-literate: A descriptive term for a doctor who treats large numbers of Lyme cases, generally with prolonged courses of antibiotics.

nymph: The third stage in the life cycle of a tick. Nymphs are extremely tiny—about the size of a poppy seed—and are responsible for most cases of Lyme disease transmission.

pathogens: Specific agents, such as viruses or bacteria, that cause a disease.

serological tests: Tests that examine a person's blood serum for antibodies to a particular pathogen.

spirochete: Any member of an order of bacteria characterized by a long spiral shape, many of which cause illness.

vector: An organism that transmits a bacterium or virus that causes a disease to another organism.

zoonosis: A disease that can be passed from animals to humans.

American Lyme Disease Foundation (ALDF)
PO Box 466
Lyme, CT 06371
executivedir@aldf.com
www.aldf.com
This organization is dedicated to the prevention, diagnosis, and treatment of Lyme disease and seeks to educate the public about the illness.

Bay Area Lyme Foundation
884 Portola Road, Suite A7
Portola Valley, CA 94028
(650) 530-2439
info@bayarealyme.org
www.bayarealyme.org
Bay Area Lyme Foundation offers tick testing and supports research and Lyme awareness.

Infectious Diseases Society of America (IDSA)
1300 Wilson Boulevard, Suite 300
Arlington, VA 22209
(703) 299-0200
www.idsociety.org
The IDSA is an organization of health care professionals who specialize in infectious diseases such as Lyme. It seeks to improve patient care and foster education and research on infectious diseases.

International Lyme and Associated Diseases Society (ILADS)
PO Box 341461
Bethesda, MD 20827
(301) 263-1080
contact@ilads.org
www.ilads.org
ILADS is a nonprofit medical society dedicated to the diagnosis and appropriate treatment of Lyme disease. Many of its directors and officers are Lyme-literate doctors.

Lyme Disease Association (LDA)
PO Box 1438
Jackson, NJ 08527
(888) 366-6611
lda@lymediseaseassociation.org
www.lymediseaseassociation.org
The LDA funds research on Lyme and seeks to educate the public about the disease.

FOR MORE INFORMATION

Books

Edlow, Jonathan A. *Bull's Eye: Unraveling the Medical Mystery of Lyme*. New Haven, CT: Yale University Press, 2003.
Edlow's book explores the discovery of Lyme disease in the United States.

Horowitz, Richard I. *Why Can't I Get Better?: Solving the Mystery of Lyme and Chronic Disease*. New York, NY: St. Martin's Press, 2013.
Dr. Horowitz writes about his diagnosis process, his treatment methods, and his clinical findings.

Squire, Ann. *Lyme Disease*. New York, NY: Children's Press, 2017.
This book gives further information about Lyme disease.

Wall, Mary. *Lyme Disease Is No Fun: Let's Get Well!* Jackson, NJ: Lyme Disease Association, 2004.
This book is written for children suffering from Lyme and focuses on helping them understand the illness and how best to cope with it.

Weintraub, Pamela. *Cure Unknown: Inside the Lyme Epidemic*. New York, NY: St. Martin's Press, 2008.
Recommended for older children, this book provides an in-depth look at the controversy over the existence of chronic Lyme.

Websites

Centers for Disease Control and Prevention: Lyme Disease
www.cdc.gov/ncidod/dvbid/lyme
This website provides general information about the transmission and treatment of Lyme disease, along with statistics of reported cases and informational guides and brochures.

Johns Hopkins University: Lyme Disease Clinical Research Center
www.hopkinsrheumatology.org/specialty-clinics/
lyme-disease-clinical-research-center/
This website contains general information about the work done by Dr. John Aucott and his team of researchers and clinicians in the advancement of Lyme disease treatment and testing.

The Lyme Disease Network
www.lymenet.org
Visitors to this website find information and news about Lyme disease as well as online and in-person support groups for people with the disease.

LymeDisease.org
www.lymedisease.org
This website includes a symptom checklist to help people determine whether they should talk to a doctor as well as contact information for Lyme-literate doctors.

INDEX

A

acrodermatitis chronica atrophicans, 31, 35

Advanced Topics in Lyme Disease (Burrascano), 83

Afzelius, Arvid, 35

American Lyme Disease Foundation (ALDF), 21, 73

animals with Lyme disease, 80

antibiotics for treatment of Lyme disease, 35, 48–50, 51–52, 56, 57, 77, 80

    debate over prolonged treatment, 65–70

    IV treatment, 50, 63–64

    prolonged treatment, 57, 60–62, 68

    risks of prolonged treatment, 63–65

antibodies, 40–41, 42–44, 62

antigens, 40, 43, 62

arthritis

    juvenile idiopathic, 22

    Lyme, 34, 49–50

Aucott, John, 83

B

babesiosis, 37–39

bacteria

    about, 10

    antibiotic resistant, 64–65

    genetic blueprint, 82

Baker, Phillip, 65

Barbour, Alan G., 17–18

Bell's palsy, 28

blood, donating, 15

blood serum, examining, 40, 42, 44, 45

Blumenthal, Richard, 67–68

Borrelia afzelii, 11, 31

Borrelia burgdorferi sensu stricto, 11–12, 14–15, 19, 31, 40, 44, 46, 56, 57, 70, 78, 79, 81, 83

    detecting DNA of for diagnosis, 47–48

    genetic blueprint of Lyme-causing bacteria, 82

ABOUT THE AUTHOR

Raymond J. Lampke resides in Buffalo, NY, and is employed in e-commerce content development. In addition to his full-time work, he is also a freelance music writer. In his spare time, he enjoys the study of historic musicology, reading, writing, and record collecting. He is also a fervent supporter of the English football club Manchester City.